Breakthrough Performance

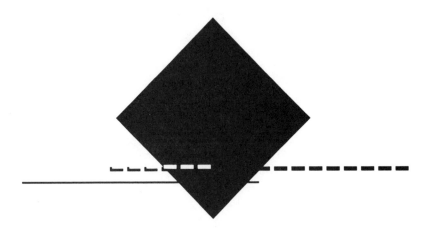

Managing for Speed and Flexibility

by

William R. Daniels

Library of Congress Catalog Card Number: 94-0072419

Copyright © 1995 by American Consulting & Training, Inc.

ACT Publishing
604 Panoramic Highway
Mill Valley, California 94941
(415) 388-6651; (800) 995-6651; FAX (415) 388-6672

Printed in the United States of America

ISBN: 1-882939-00-X

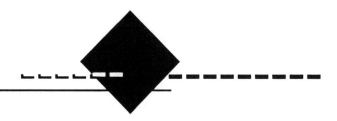

Acknowledgments

◆ ◆ ◆ ◆

This book has been in the making for several years and is based on much of my consulting work. Many people have influenced this particular manuscript. Although it is impossible for me to list everyone involved, I would like to acknowledge a few key contributors.

First, of course, is Lila Sparks-Daniels, the President of American Consulting & Training (ACT) and my wife. She has been the most persistent influence and coworker—she has helped form the book's strategy and graphics; she has edited and rewritten; she has offered her encouragement and advice all along the way at just the right times; and she has quite gracefully killed two entire earlier drafts and nursed me through the grief so that I could carry on again to the final product!

Bernard Johann was a great sounding board in the early stages of the book's development and in later phases of evaluation. Billie Riboli and John Mathers of ACT have been a constant support. Thanks also to friends Bill and Kathy Baxter for the generous use of their inspiring Sea Ranch beach home.

Graham Core, Theresa Fenske and Patricia Wiggenhorn of Professional Resources & Communications, Inc. have made the book happen. Their editing, book design and other assistance in publishing have been essential and are very much appreciated.

Writing always provokes one's memory—a recital of influential working relationships. While writing this book, Emanuel Kay, Donald Tosti and Bob Carleton often seemed to be peering over my shoulder.

More recent memories come from the hundreds of managers and individual contributors in client organizations, especially in Intel; Motorola; SEMATECH; Northwestern Mutual Life Insurance; Levi Strauss & Co.; the City of Oakland, California; Baxter International; and Norwest Corporation, Minneapolis.

This book is a snapshot of what I have learned from my colleagues. Thank you all.

Contents

Preface

◆ ◆ ◆ ◆

This book is for the *real managers* at work—the individual contributors—and their bosses who want to encourage them to be more proactive. With flatter and flatter organizations demanding more speed and flexibility, *everyone must manage themselves*.

My hope is that middle managers and first-line managers (supervisors) will use this book to improve the management skills of their first-line employees. The work of the organization is not managed by those called "managers." For the most part, work is managed by those who do the work. Until employees manage more effectively, the efforts of "managers" are wasted.

It has taken me more than 20 years to learn who manages the organization. Those years were spent consulting exclusively with those formally identified as the managers—at Intel, SEMATECH, Motorola and Levi Strauss & Co., at Northwestern Mutual Life Insurance in Milwaukee, with Norwest Corporation, with Baxter Healthcare Corporation, with Schering Plough and Bristol Myers-Squibb in New Jersey, with Bank of America and with many cities, counties and schools of California. We were well-intentioned, and we worked hard at both learning the new methods of management and applying them to actual work. But the return on our efforts never seemed great enough. Getting our ideas out of the classroom and then out of the managers' offices into the work always distorted and diminished our effects.

Results began to change several years ago, when Intel invited my company to design a simulation for teaching performance management skills to first-line managers. The Chain Gang Simulation calls for the manufacture of two kinds of paper chain. During a five-minute production run, orders are determined by the role of dice and filled within very demanding constraints of cost and quality. The full day of training includes four production runs during which the teams attempt to make money producing their chains. Only about 40 percent of the teams ever break even. But some are extraordinarily profitable.

At the end of each round, the quiet concentration of the winning teams erupts into a noisy spontaneous celebration—victory shouts, applause, high fives, even little "touchdown" dances! Morale is obviously high, and the team members show all the signs of mutual trust, confidence and respect. But it isn't this respect and enthusiasm that determine the difference. Other teams display similar enthusiasm even when the final quality inspection and accounting indicate that they have had another bad round.

What makes the extraordinary teams so different? That is the lesson to which everyone turns their attention. We always find the same answer. The people who actually handle materials during the five-minute round are so well-informed and practiced in their performance that they manage themselves. They work to very specific standards for pace and quality. These people know (can recall with accuracy) exactly how they are doing within every 15-second time period. And they can take corrective action alone or with other teammates to put themselves back on track when problems arise. These extraordinary teams work in the conditions we describe in this book as the Breakthrough System.

Other members of the team who "supervise" the work take on roles of information providers, contingency planners, sources of pace and quality feedback. But the amazing thing is how quiet and calm these winning teams get as their performance breaks through. The members talk to each other very efficiently during the production runs—a word of thanks, a simple piece of advice, announcements of their accomplishments and problems—as they deliver their world-class, zero-defect production and profitability.

Between production runs, team meetings are intense! There is hardly enough air time for everyone to talk. *Workers* and *supervisors* are indistinguishable as participants. Everyone takes responsibility for the performance of the team, and everyone gives and takes encouragement and advice. Talk is clearly focused on clarifying the goals, correcting processes and establishing individual performance expectations. And winning teams conduct their discussions *while they practice!* The meetings are clearly a time for both decision making and learning.

All day long, the winning teams display the characteristics of brilliant management. They are small organizations with clear, common goals. Everyone is fully authorized to influence their part of the organization's performance. They excel in learning from their successes and their problems. They invent contingency responses that allow them to adjust to a wide range of unpredictable demands from their environment. And they win—they produce greater volumes of high-quality chains than the teams with less brilliant management. They are focused, flat, fast, flexible human organizations.

After running this simulation with hundreds of teams at Intel, Motorola and many other organizations (most recently the leadership program for the public high schools in Alaska), it finally became apparent that performance management skills were being taught to the wrong population. Or perhaps we were teaching these skills to a much too limited population. The workshop participants (first-line managers) pointed out that the people who most use performance management skills are those who do the work. They recognized that managers are not the *coaches* of work nearly as much as are the workers themselves. Managers can't control the work environment as well as the workers. Safety, quality and cost effectiveness can't be managed any better than they are managed by those who produce the results for customers—the first-line employees.

So now, first line managers are using the Chain Gang Simulation to teach performance management skills to the members of the work teams they lead. It is no surprise that the same results and enthusiasm are exhibited by the individual contributors during the workshop. But they respond to the workshop in three ways that *are* different. First, individual contributors (such as equipment operators and engineers) show even more appreciation for the performance management skills. Secondly, they are usually a little surprised and then delighted that their power to manage is being acknowledged and encouraged. Finally, they are both able and insistent upon immediately applying the management skills. They talk to each other and their managers about all the principles and begin planning how they will use the skills on the next shift. A fire is lit that burns immediately in relationship to real work. The group commits!

Clearly, the right people for Breakthrough skills are those who do the organization's work. They are the ones whose concern and self-discipline make the big difference in the way our organizations are managed. And their readiness to improve the way they've been managing our organizations is very exciting. It's as though these people have been waiting for a long time to get on with it.

Breakthrough Performance is a presentation of the ideas covered briefly in the lectures I've offered in various performance management workshops. Employees and their managers have been asking for these chapters for some time. My hope is that first-line managers will make time in their regular meetings, perhaps monthly, to use one or more of the chapters to promote their group's thinking about how they are managing themselves.

As management improves where it matters most—among those who do the work—our organizations will become *change able*. Such organizations are essential if we are to be *response able* to the opportunities of this time in history. The new information economy, driven by the hardware and software of communications technology and the services that these new tools make possible, presents us with an extraordinary opportunity to improve the quality of human life. This is no longer the dream of futurists, it is a present reality.

We actualize the information economy by working smarter. We insist on clear performance expectations, immediate and reliable feedback about how our current performance compares to those expectations and control over the resources necessary to achieve those expectations. And this positions us as individuals for extraordinary cooperation with others—as we work side by side and sit together in meetings. Working smarter makes our organizations *change able, response able* and *profit able.*

Working smart to make our organizations change able is not easy. We must also work hard—suffering in ways that make us sweat and worry. We already know that the change able organization and the information economy do not alleviate all the suffering of work. But they make the process of delivering products and services to customers more immediate and personal. We get to know how our customers use our outputs, and this contributes directly to the quality of our lives. This knowledge allows us to make an informed judgment about the meaningfulness of our work. Quality of life is measured in both the quantity of its pleasure and the meaningfulness of its suffering.

May this book contribute to your good work and the quality of your life.

William R. Daniels
Mill Valley, California

Section

I

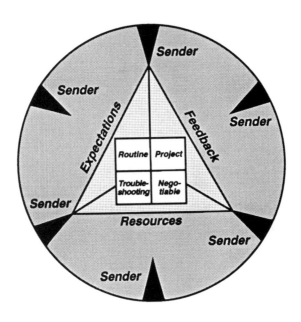

The Essential Concepts of Breakthrough Performance

Who Cares?
Your Role Set

♦ ♦ ♦ ♦

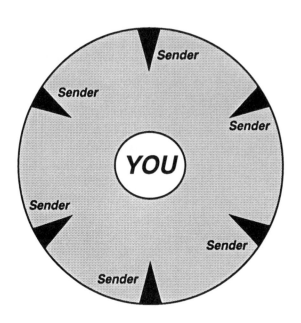

Overview

Most of us think that management is done by people who occupy the upper stories of an organization's hierarchy—those with the job title *manager*. Not true. Management is, in fact, done by workers *at the bottom*, on the *front lines*. Those who do an organization's day-to-day work are the people who manage an organization's performance. *Breakthrough Performance—Managing for Speed and Flexibility* is about improving management for the people who actually manage the work that organizations do.

Front-line workers have always been the actual managers. We manage ourselves, and we manage each other. We need to become conscious of our power and responsibility for management; our economic survival depends on it. To continue improving our standard of living and our quality of life, we must make our organizations more effective at creating and delivering their products and services. Better management is needed in manufacturing and retail businesses; it's also necessary in our schools, hospitals and government offices. Since we're the ones who manage these organizations, it's up to us.

In this first chapter, we introduce the informal system that really manages our organizations. This system is composed of *Role Sets*—small groups of people who depend on one another to get things done. These are the vital few people who really matter to each of us at work.

By paying attention to these relationships, we accomplish everything that matters at work. By understanding and skillfully using the system of Role Sets, each of us can realize greater power over our own jobs. By learning to cooperate effectively with the members of our Role Sets, we can improve the quality and efficiency of the work we do. We can also establish mutual support systems that recognize and encourage everyone's contributions to the work. We build our own reputations for competence and reliability by taking care of our Role Sets, and diminish the distress and frustration that we often feel at work.

The next chapters of this book discuss the specific conditions we need to be highly productive. These are conditions we have to create in cooperation with our Role Sets. Chapter 2 focuses on the importance of clear expectations, reliable feedback and adequate control of resources. Chapter 3 explains the Basic Systems Model and the

Task Grid, two tools for understanding and managing specific tasks that make up our work.

Chapters 4 through 6 describe the process of taking a job apart and putting it back together, task by task, to assure that we can manage ourselves in Breakthrough Systems.

Chapters 7 and 8 cover specific methods for gaining support and understanding from our Role Set. By that point, we will know exactly what to say to get these critical few people to make their expectations clear and realistic and to drive covert conflict into the open where we can work to resolve it. Chapter 8 gives special attention to ways that we can use meetings to manage these vital working relationships.

Finally, Chapters 9 and 10 explore ways to accelerate work-related learning and change.

All of us want our organizations to be better managed. It's up to us—let's get busy.

Key Concepts

- ♦ The complexity, pace and demands for quality are increasing, so we must manage our work better.
- ♦ Work is managed by those of us who do it. We are responsible for managing ourselves and one another.
- ♦ Role Sets are the informal systems that we use to manage each other.
- ♦ When we fail to manage our Role Sets well, role ambiguity, role conflict and role overload cause great distress.

Possible Activities

- ♦ Identify the people and expectations that comprise our Role Set.
- ♦ Identify some of the causes of distress in our Role Set.

Who Is Really Managing?

Our economy is suffering from the effects of poor management. We have amazing computerized technology to help us become more productive, but in many sectors of our economy, productivity has been at a near standstill for the past 20 years. Manufacturing, agriculture and mining operations have made significant strides; they've become more efficient with automation and high-powered, precision equipment. But these jobs represent a small portion of our total economy. Nearly 70 percent of American jobs now involve providing information and services.

Businesses in the service sector have spent more than a trillion dollars over the past two decades on phones, computers, fax machines and photocopiers, in an attempt to increase efficiency. They've also spent enormous sums training workers to use these devices. Nearly three whole generations of workers have become computer-literate.

New technologies are emerging all the time—enormously powerful personal computers, laptops and palmtops and brilliant new software systems. As computers get more powerful and complex, they are also getting easier to use. To date, however, the return on our massive investment in technology has been disappointingly low.

Poor productivity means, in many cases, that our paychecks are barely increasing—sometimes our pay is actually cut. Even if our pay is holding steady, its value is being eaten away by inflation. We're working harder and longer, but we're experiencing less and less satisfaction, and we have less to show for our efforts. The wear and tear is exhibiting itself in both physical and emotional exhaustion.

Bad Management Is Real and Persisting

We all seem to know that management is to blame. Every time anyone listens to us, we say so. Sociologists and industrial psychologists have been building a database of our complaints for more than 40 years. The books *Working* by Studs Terkel, and *The Cynical Americans* by Donald Kanter and Philip Mirvis, are just two of many popular chronicles of frustration and rage at management. We blame management because we are bored, lack authority and feel like disposable cogs in the machinery. We complain about outmoded bureaucratic rituals and managers caught up in pointless power games and personal greed. Our nervous systems are overloaded by constant demands for more work, different work and better work. People inside our organizations and customers outside send us more and more messages about their dissatisfaction with our performance. Life at work seems less and less predictable, secure or satisfying. Despite our protests, our distress at work seems to be increasing.

How could any manager ignore the need for improvement or have difficulty finding help? Every year, organizations spend billions of dollars on management development programs. The management section of retail bookstores is one of the fastest-growing segments of the publishing business. Management consultants are springing up everywhere. Why isn't management—and all the management advice now available—solving the management problems of poor productivity and work-related stress?

The answer is that we've been sending our complaints and our management-development resources to the *wrong people*. We've forgotten who *the management* really is.

Consider the evidence:

Workers talk about work to somebody in a formal management role only *twice a day* on the average. The total amount of time involved in these contacts is rarely more than four minutes. But workers talk to one another about work *20 times an hour*—almost constantly.

Workers carry the giant's share of management in every organization. The evidence is not new—as far as anyone knows, this is how work has always been managed. It is not an ideal to strive for; it is past and current *reality*. Front-line workers perform the key functions and activities usually identified as management—setting goals, facilitating work, building supportive relations and leading teams.

Proponents of *scientific management* made the novel suggestion a century ago that all these activities should be the specialty of people at the upper levels of a hierarchy. But that separation has been more a matter of theory than practice. The management of the organization and its performance of work have always remained in the hands of the people *doing* the work.

This does not mean that a century of theorizing and research about management is irrelevant. The massive effort to understand how people cooperate in complex structures to produce the extraordinary technological gains of the 20th century have built a great treasure of information. This research has uncovered many new and better ways to manage work. More is known about management functions and their importance than ever before, and we desperately need this knowledge.

Victims or Managers: We Must Choose

Unfortunately, in the process of collecting and sharing this information, we have created and maintained an illusion that management is a specialty reserved for those with titles like *supervisor, manager, director* and *executive.* This illusion has led us to focus both our complaints and our corrective actions on the wrong people. We must take our knowledge and complaints about management to those who can and must translate it into action: ourselves—the *workers, employees, individual contributors, associates.* Those of us who perform the organization's work need to recognize *ourselves* as the actual managers. We are the ones who must solve the management problem.

No doubt we will continue designating a few among us to specialize in the tasks of coordinating and supervising the work of our groups. We will empower these people to make decisions on our behalf, so our efforts can be coordinated on a large scale. This is the real purpose of the information network called a *hierarchy.* Hierarchy was a great invention, and over the past 5,000 years we've learned a lot about how to make it work. Information technology allows us to use this old invention even more effectively.

We've also learned how to protect ourselves from hierarchy's abuses. We know that whenever we operate in the illusion that hierarchy has a monopoly on management functions, we permit it to abuse us.

Too many of us have been participating in the illusion that bosses manage while we just do what we're told. Bosses are supposed to bark, and we are supposed to jump. It easily deteriorates to a relationship in which we see *them* as the bad people and ourselves as the good people who are *victims* of our bosses. As long as everybody plays these roles, our organizations sort of work. And employees can pretend that all the organization's problems are their *bosses'* fault.

This old illusion is cracking up under tremendous new pressures:

◆ The information revolution is pushing us into a new world of speed and continuous change.

◆ The demand is rising for products and services that are perfect in quality.

◆ New global markets and new competitors are putting pressure on prices.

Are We Victims or Managers?

Victim	**Manager**
Work relationships as	Work relationships as
hazard	***support group***
• We see ourselves as helpless. • We blame others for our own behavior and feelings. • We are resentful and appear to be unhappy.	• We take responsibility for the conditions in which we work. • We keep expectations clear. • We drive conflict into the open so negotiation can take place. • We insist on realistic expectations—something ordinary human beings can accomplish given the resources, including time, skill and energy.
but	
• We are content that our life is in other peoples' hands. • We live with and support the illusion that others are responsible for our well-being.	

Voice of the Victim	**Voice of the Manager**
"When are they going to get this place organized?"	"How can I help get this place better organized?"
"Nobody gives a care about anybody else around here—it's everyone for herself!"	"I'm responsible for how I work with others."
"It's not my job to reason why; I just do what I'm told."	"I insist on understanding the big picture—the strategy as well as the tactics."
"What I'm doing doesn't make sense to me, but if I stop doing it this way, I'll get in trouble; so let someone else figure it out."	"Doing work always involves some suffering; but I am responsible for minimizing the suffering while staying focused on our goals."

Playing our old roles makes our organizations slow and unintelligent in responding to these pressures. Organizations can no longer afford poor cooperation between "labor" and "management." To survive, organizations cannot change in long, slow turns like a huge ship. Instead, organizations must be able to turn instantly in response to threats and opportunities—like a school of fish. Each of us must be able to change our role quickly as the needs and opportunities arise. And the changes we make in our own performance have to be perfectly coordinated with everyone else. This means that there must be good management everywhere in the organization. It specifically means that those of us who do the organization's work must take our management responsibilities more seriously.

Until we do this, our productivity will remain low and our quality of life will remain in a stall. Until we acknowledge ourselves as the primary practitioners of management, we will continue to experience distress at work and silence in response to our complaints. We can choose to manage, or watch our organizations fail, our work disappear and our quality of life deteriorate.

It *is* time to improve management—to improve *ourselves*. It's time *we* improved the way we relate to one another at work. We won't get rid of hierarchy, and we won't burn the management books. Instead, we must make hierarchy a better servant and use all the management knowledge to improve our performance and cooperation. We begin the necessary change by changing ourselves—by accepting our role as manager.

How We Manage: The Informal System of Role Sets

Improving our performance as managers means that we must change our roles at work. The word *role* is another way of saying *pattern of behavior*. To change our roles means we will be attempting to change our pattern of behavior.

As soon we attempt to alter our behavior, we will run up against the real system that manages us at work. We usually participate in it without thinking. It is subtle and nearly invisible. It is often referred to as the *informal system of management*. But despite its subtlety and informality, it is very powerful.

Role Set

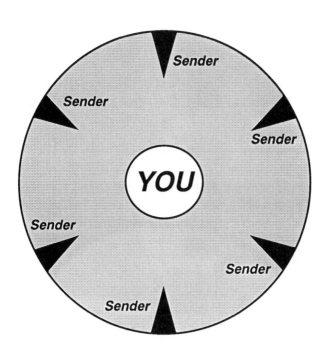

Role Senders

This powerful system of management comes to light as we discover that our behavior at work—our role—is never a private matter. Others see themselves depending on our behavior. They expect us to do certain things and become irritated and alarmed when we don't meet their expectations. Those who know that they depend on us make themselves an influence on us. Our behavior—our role—is shaped by the influence of others and becomes the result of a special kind of group agreement. We find that changing our roles is not something we are allowed to do alone.

People who see themselves as dependent upon us send us all kinds of messages about how satisfied they are with our behavior. Most of these messages are nonverbal—facial expressions, body postures and gestures. Sometimes the messages are verbal—sentences, phrases, sighs or groans. Occasionally the messages are written down. In whatever form, however, these messages usually indicate approval or disapproval, more-or-less subtle promises or threats—rewards or punishments. Often, the messages are only signs of approval or disapproval that don't say clearly what we did that the sender liked or disliked.

Those who depend on some part of our behavior and send us messages about their level of satisfaction are called *role senders*. By sending their threats and promises, our role senders teach us what they want. They send us information about a piece of the role that we must play if we want to avoid their punishments and earn their rewards. They teach us our role. Their expectations—and their ability to make us take them seriously—are what make them role senders.

We usually have more than one role sender at work. But these role senders don't recognize one another, so no one can explain ahead of time the whole system of expectations that will affect us in our job. When we take a new job, especially one that was previously held by someone else, the invisible management system is already in place, waiting to make itself known to us.

This becomes obvious when we do something that disappoints one or more of our role senders. Then we get a message that says "Stop that!" These "stop" messages show us who our role senders are and eventually lead us to at least a rough understanding of which behavior they will tolerate.

We often find surprises when we attempt to identify our actual role senders. We discover that peers have more influence over our day-to-day behavior than our boss—or that a clerk in the mail room is more important than the person standing next to us on the job. But there are reliable characteristics—clues—that identify role senders:

◆ Role senders think that they depend on our performance.

◆ Role senders can usually reach us within 30 minutes.

◆ We often have especially negative relationships with role senders; they threaten and irritate us.

Role Sets

At work, each of us usually has three to five role senders—rarely more than eight. As a group, these people are known as our Role Set. Over time, this Role Set causes us to find ways to repeat the behaviors that they want and to avoid the behaviors that they don't want. We serve the needs of our Role Set through a pattern of behavior that avoids their disapproval and punishment and earns their approval and rewards. This pattern of behavior changes in predictable ways, depending on which members of the Role Set are paying attention to our performance at any given time. The combined effect of all the role senders' messages is our role—a stable pattern of behavior.

Role Sets are the structure of the *informal* system of management in any organization, and this system is seldom consistent with the organization's formal organization chart. So we learn about it through trial and error over a period of about three months. We eventually find a pattern of behavior that doesn't provoke many negative messages from our Role Set. This pattern of behavior is our real role in the organization, and it may be quite different from our formal job description. It also may be different from the role that we wanted when we accepted the job. But we usually learn the hard way that the role expected by our Role Set is the one that we have to perform. It seems to be the only way to get along, to avoid punishment and to get support.

Some people are so sensitive to Role Set messages that they slip into their roles without even noticing the process. Those of us who are less sensitive experience the process as distressing and unpleasant—the role senders turn the volume and heat up on their messages until we pay attention and make the required responses. If we ignore our role senders, if we "just don't get it," the Role Set usually gets us fired or makes us so miserable that we quit. Getting along with our Role Set is very serious business.

A worksheet is included on page 21 to help us identify our own Role Sets.

Being a Role Sender

So far, we've only discussed how the Role Set system affects us as *receivers* of role sender messages. But we are also role senders to others. We participate in influencing the behaviors of others.

Each of us depends on at least one or two other people in the organization to help us perform our role successfully. For instance, we need information from our supervisors, materials, supplies and cooperation and support from some of our fellow workers. Sometimes the people we depend upon also depend upon us; we are interdependent and operate as role senders to each other. But this is not always the case. Sometimes we depend upon others who don't seem to know that we exist!

After being on the job for about six months, we've usually figured out who we depend on. We have also discovered how to get the people we depend upon to pay attention to our needs. We've found out what we can do to reward or punish these people, and we use this knowledge to influence their behavior. We become role senders for these people and send our messages of approval and disapproval in order to get the cooperation we need.

Some of us are pretty rough—we jerk hard on other people's chains to get their attention—while others are smoother and more graceful. Our styles are usually determined by our own Role Sets. We are expected to play rough; we get roughed up if we don't. Or we're expected to be polite and graceful—and our Role Sets politely cut our heads off if we're not. The organization's culture—its real norms and values—is determined and maintained by the continuous exchange of messages between role senders and role receivers.

The Stabilizing Effect of Role Sets

The Role-Set structure of an organization resembles a giant fishnet. Each knot in the net represents an individual. Each individual is tied to a few others. If we grab hold of any one individual within the system and pull hard, sooner or later we will lift the whole net out of the water—or tear it to useless shreds.

Role Sets link together to make a network of social dependencies. Any change in one individual's behavior affects the behavior of everyone else—some more than others, but everyone to some degree. To change an individual role, we must change the whole organization; to change the organization, we must change every individual's role.

This complex net of interdependencies makes the organization a stable system. Any time we start to change, our Role Set says: "Wait a minute! Does this mean we can't count on you as usual? If we can't count on you, we won't be able to satisfy our Role Sets, and they will punish us. And then we'll punish you!" We get this message and usually decide that change isn't such a good idea.

This stabilizing effect has both a positive and a negative side. On the positive side, it is a very effective way to make our behavior constant and predictable, and this is essential to human cooperation.

When our personal goals, our Role Set's expectations and the organization's overall mission are aligned, the Role Set functions as a very effective support group for each of us. Furthermore, Role Sets protect the organization from the anarchy that results when people start "doing their own thing." And Role Sets protect the organization from tyranny by any individual. In the Role-Set system, no one person can shove everybody else around. Everyone is subject to influence by others and in turn, influences others.

On the negative side, Role Sets can make everyone fear change. If we know that others depend on us to act in a consistent way—and that they can and will punish us if we don't—we are smart to be slow and careful about changing our behavior. This makes it difficult for an organization to respond quickly when new threats or opportunities emerge. An organization may keep doing business as usual until it suddenly discovers that there is no business left to do. Only as each of us becomes skillful and deliberate in managing our Role-Set relationships can we increase their supportive function and avoid their distressing and rigidifying effects.

How Our Mismanagement Hurts Us: Role Set Problems

When we don't manage our Role Sets well, they create distressful situations for us. Such distress is a symptom of poor management going on within this powerful, informal system. There are three common ways in which Role Sets cause us distress, and it is helpful to recognize these Role-Set problems:

1. **Role Ambiguity**—uncertainty about what our role senders expect;
2. **Role Conflict**—being caught between two inherently contradictory expectations; and
3. **Role Overload**—operating under a set of expectations that we simply cannot satisfy because we don't have the time or energy.

When we find these problems operating in our Role Set, we must start negotiating like crazy! None of these three situations is creative or productive, so the sooner we can eliminate them, the sooner we will have better working relationships. (Chapter 7 includes specific suggestions about how to conduct these negotiations. This chapter will simply help identify role senders and the stress points in our Role-Set relationships.)

Role Ambiguity

> *"Every time I mention doing a customer survey, Bill groans and rolls his eyes or sighs—then the group quickly moves on to some other subject."*
>
> *"I got the 'Employee of the Month Award,' but I don't understand why. I was just doing my job as usual; why this unusual recognition?"*

We experience *Role Ambiguity* when we aren't sure what our role senders expect. We get messages—punishments and rewards—about whether or not our senders are satisfied, but we aren't sure which behaviors provoke these responses. It's like walking in a mine field—every step is a risky guess. If we just stand still, though, we could find that we are standing on a mine with a delayed fuse!

Role Ambiguity wears us out with anxiety. The first step in reducing Role Ambiguity is to identify the members of our Role Set and then get them thinking and talking about what they want from us. We need their understanding and support. (See Chapter 7 for more about negotiating with your Role Set.)

Role Conflict

> *"Don told me to go to Arizona to help with the computer-maintenance problem. Now the Finance Department won't approve my expenses. They say that the trip wasn't properly authorized. I could be out 800 bucks!"*
>
> *"On Monday, Frank asked me to attend Doris's meetings, which are held every morning from 9 to 10 a.m. On Wednesday, Frank asked me to make a presentation in his staff meeting, which is held on Mondays at 9 a.m. I can't do both—what does he really want?"*

When members of our Role Set have contradictory expectations, we are caught in *Role Conflict.* Usually, these contradictory expectations are held by two *different* role senders. For instance, one sender wants us to describe how an accident happened; another wants us to keep quiet. But sometimes a single role sender has contradictory expectations—this is a real *crazy maker*. Sometimes we try to escape the situation by satisfying whichever role sender (or expectation) is most pressing at the moment. Then, when that situation isn't so urgent, we try to take care of the other. Eventually, however, the two are likely to collide, and we get whacked by both.

If we can anticipate Role Conflict, we can make it less stressful. Most sales work, for instance, constantly positions us between what our organization wants to make and the price it wants to charge, and what our customers want and are willing to pay. The whole point of the salesperson's role is to resolve this conflict. We can anticipate it and develop the conflict-resolution skills called *selling*. Under these conditions, instead of finding the role distressing, some of us find it exhilarating!

But Role Conflict is dangerous when it catches us by surprise, when it is *covert*. It feels like we're being tackled from behind when we didn't even know that we were carrying the ball. If covert Role Conflict happens frequently, it can drive up our blood pressure and pop our hearts.

As with Role Ambiguity, the first step in reducing covert Role Conflict is to drive it into the open. Then we can define it, negotiate about it and develop the skills for resolving it. This process requires that we know who the members of our Role Set are and how to seek their understanding and support.

Role Overload

> *"I'm expected to verify 75 circuit devices per week, but the software tool will only handle 50 at best. Nobody's making another computer or faster software available—how can I succeed?"*
>
> *"Doris wants me to attend a half-day meeting Thursday; Ernie demanded that I have three more projects completed by Friday. It's Tuesday afternoon—when will I get any sleep?"*

Overload is the distress that we notice most often. The expectations are clear and compatible; the problem is that too much is expected. We don't have enough time in the day or energy in our bodies to get it all done.

If we try to solve this problem by just working harder, we usually wear out. Fatigue is a subtle pain. The young hardly notice it—a night's sleep removes all the symptoms. But the wear and tear that fatigue causes is real and becomes more noticeable later in life. In the meantime, we worry about all the work still undone. We take it home in our briefcases, in our hearts and in our minds.

We become dull and boring to our family and friends, because we are always tied up in our work. We slowly isolate ourselves from the rest of our lives, only to find that no amount of effort and time is enough to catch up with our workload. We tend to find pleasure and peace of mind only through escapism, such as watching television compulsively and abusing substances, from food to illegal drugs. This pattern of behavior is now recognized as *burnout* or workaholism. It is a common form of self-destruction.

The trap closes around us when we respond to Role Overload by trying to work harder. In fact, there will always be more work than we are able to do. The only way to increase productivity and also keep work in proper perspective is to work smarter. We must clarify our Role Set's expectations, stay focused on the real priorities and learn or invent shortcuts to achieve these few key results. We must take the initiative to begin acting this way individually, and the first step is to seek understanding and support from our Role Set.

Each of the three Role-Set problems can cause specific physical problems for us. Medical research has shown that ambiguity can lead to cancer and digestive pathologies, such as ulcers and inflamed intestines. Frequent surprise conflict can drive up one's blood pressure and cause heart attacks and strokes. Overload often leads to burnout—feelings of powerlessness and meaninglessness, depression and substance abuse. Whether or not we manage our Roles Sets well is literally a matter of life and death.

Your Turn: Identifying and Evaluating Your Role Set

The following worksheet can help you identify who is in your Role Set, what you already know about their expectations and what kinds of distress you currently experience in these relationships. (To assist you in using the *Role Set Analysis Worksheet,* a sample of a completed analysis appears on page 23.)

Directions for completing the worksheet:

1. Before you use the worksheet, make a list of people that *might be* in your role set—people who have the following relationship to you at work:

   - People who perceive themselves as dependent upon some part of your performance—if you don't do it, they believe that they will get in trouble.

   - People who tend to know where you are all the time—they are able to reach you within any 30-minute period.

   - People who are able to get your attention because they can use their influence on your behalf; reward you with approval and positive attention; or can threaten, irritate or harm you in some way.

2. If your list has more than five names, pick the five that best fit all the criteria and enter them on the worksheet.

3. Spread 100 points among these five names to indicate their relative importance as role senders. For example, if you have five role senders who are equally important, give each name 20 points. If some senders are more important than others, give them higher points than others.

4. Under each name, list what you are *sure* this person expects of you—i.e., depends on you to do. If you are not sure, then write what you *guess* is expected and add a question mark.

   - List expectations that are specifically work-related.

   - List other behaviors that are important to this person— e.g., going out for drinks after work.

5. Distribute the points that you assigned to each name among that person's expectations to show which expectations you think are most important. For example: if you assigned a person 20 points in Step 3, and that person has 2 expectations—one of which is much more important than the other— you might assign 15 points to that person's most important expectation and 5 points to the less important expectation.

   Note: The best way to determine the importance of each expectation is to consider which ones carry the most potential for rewards or punishments from that sender.

Note: When following directions 6–8, use the letter of the "sender" followed by the number of that sender's expectation and its priority weight to fill in the blanks. For example, you will refer to the first expectation of the first sender as A, 1 (plus priority weight). You may find it appropriate to list the same expectations in more than one place.

6. In the space labeled *Ambiguities*, list the Role Senders and the expectations with question marks that you assigned in Step 4. Add the priority weights of all these ambiguous expectations to get your *Ambiguity Score.*

7. In the space labeled *Conflicts*, list side-by-side all the Role Senders and the expectations that contradict one another. Put a check mark next to the conflicts that are *covert*—catch you by surprise when they happen. Only add the priority weights of all the expectations involved in these *covert conflicts* to get your *Conflict Score.*

8. In the space labeled *Overload*, list all the Role Senders and the expectations that you don't think you will ever have the time, energy, skills or resources to satisfy. Add the priority weights of all these expectations to get your *Overload Score.*

9. Reflect on these Charts and Lists. You should be able to see how these expectations affect how you feel and behave at work. On a separate sheet of paper, write a few paragraphs to describe how your current behavior—your role performance— attempts to satisfy your role set. In other words, describe the pattern of behavior you are using to avoid the punishments and get the rewards of your Role Senders.

Role Set Analysis Worksheet

Role Sender A (Direction 2)	Weight (D-3)	Sender A's Expectations (Direction 4)	Weight (D-5)

1. _____
2. _____
3. _____
4. _____
5. _____

Role Sender B (Direction 2)	Weight (D-3)	Sender B's Expectations (Direction 4)	Weight (D-5)

1. _____
2. _____
3. _____
4. _____
5. _____

Role Sender C (Direction 2)	Weight (D-3)	Sender C's Expectations (Direction 4)	Weight (D-5)

1. _____
2. _____
3. _____
4. _____
5. _____

Role Sender D (Direction 2)	Weight (D-3)	Sender D's Expectations (Direction 4)	Weight (D-5)

1. _____
2. _____
3. _____
4. _____
5. _____

Role Sender E (Direction 2)	Weight (D-3)	Sender E's Expectations (Direction 4)	Weight (D-5)

1. _____
2. _____
3. _____
4. _____
5. _____

Role Set Analysis Worksheet–continued

Ambiguous Expectation (Direction 6)	Weight	Conflicting Expectations (Direction 7)				Covert Weight	Overload Expectation (Direction 8)	Weight
		Expectation	Weight	Expectation	Weight			

Ambiguity Score		Covert Conflict Score		Overload Score	

20-50 Be Concerned
50 + Serious

10-30 Be Concerned
30 + Serious

20-50 Be Concerned
50 + Serious

In the space below write how your current behavior on the job attempts to satisfy these expectations. *(Direction 9)*

Roy's Role Set Analysis Worksheet

Role Sender A (Direction 2)	Weight (D-3)	Sender A's Expectations (Direction 4)	Weight (D-5)
Albert	40		
		1. Be on time.	10
		2. Keep up with the grill orders—450 pieces a night.	10
		3. Don't get complaints—make rare steaks rare & hot.	10
		4. Be nice to the waiters & waitresses?	5
		5. Leave the grill area shining clean.	5

Role Sender B (Direction 2)	Weight (D-3)	Sender B's Expectations (Direction 4)	Weight (D-5)
Betty	30		
		1. Be car-pool partner for commute to work.	10
		2. Coordinate grill orders with her salad & veg. prep.	5
		3. Help her keep the waitresses & waiters in line?	5
		4. Get through with work on time for commute home.	10
		5.	

Role Sender C (Direction 2)	Weight (D-3)	Sender C's Expectations (Direction 4)	Weight (D-5)
Carman	15		
		1. Move her orders up when she forgets to put them in.	8
		2. Be real polite—don't act *macho*.	7
		3.	
		4.	
		5.	

Role Sender D (Direction 2)	Weight (D-3)	Sender D's Expectations (Direction 4)	Weight (D-5)
Doug	10		
		1. Stop everything for the big dinner parties he serves?	4
		2. Add 50 steaks to the normal load.	4
		3. Don't let Carman push me around—don't be a wimp?	2
		4.	
		5.	

Role Sender E (Direction 2)	Weight (D-3)	Sender E's Expectations (Direction 4)	Weight (D-5)
Ed	5		
		1. Don't *ever* put someone else in front of his orders.	5
		2.	
		3.	
		4.	
		5.	

Roy's Role Set Analysis Worksheet–continued

Ambiguous Expectation (Direction 6)	Weight	Conflicting Expectations (Direction 7) Expectation	Weight	Expectation	Weight	Covert Weight	Overload Expectation (Direction 8)	Weight
A, 4	5	A, 1	10	B, 1	10	20	A, 2	10
B, 3	5	A, 4	5	B, 3	5	10	A, 3	10
D, 1	4	A, 4	5	D, 3	2		D, 1	4
D, 3	2	A, 4	5	E, 1	5			
		A, 5	5	B, 4	10			
		B, 3	5	C, 1	8	13		
		C, 1	8	D, 1	4	12		
		C, 1	8	E, 1	5	13		
		C, 2	7	D, 3	2			
		D, 1	4	E, 1	5			

Ambiguity Score	16		Covert Conflict Score	68	Overload Score	24
20-50 Be Concerned			10-30 Be Concerned		20-50 Be Concerned	
50 + Serious			30 + Serious		50 + Serious	

In the space below write how your current behavior on the job attempts to satisfy these expectations. *(Direction 9)*

My work day sometimes starts with conflict if Betty isn't ready when I drop by to pick her up for work. We both show up late, which really puts Albert in a panic and a rage. I think he blames me for her problems getting out of the house—he expects me to get both of us to work on time. But I don't know how to get Betty's kids to cooperate.

From the moment I arrive, there's a lot of work to do! I have to work fast; keep the nine different cuts of meat cooked to the exact level of rare (five different levels); make all the pieces of meat that go with one order come off at the same time (got to be hot); and stay in step with Betty's part of the order. For at least three hours each night, I have 40–70 different cuts cooking at the same time for about 12 different orders. It takes a lot of concentration. There are seven to ten waiters and waitresses I have to keep up with, and I do well with most of them.

But then there's Carmen! Drives me nuts! Can't remember to bring her orders in right when she gets them and then she wants me to "save her" by putting her orders in front of everybody else. And I have to act like I like it—she has a strong relationship with Albert (he thinks she walks water) and she puts him on my case if I don't take care of her. But Albert isn't but half of the problem. When I take care of Carmen, everyone else gets on my case. Betty snarls, Doug snickers—unless he's got a big dinner party going—then he roars, and Ed actually tries to pick a fight! It's hard to keep my mind on the steaks, and its real hard to be nice to people when you're in the middle of a war!

I end the day exhausted, and I can barely keep from screaming at Betty when she whines about my taking so long to clean up and get started on the commute home.

Summary: Let's Straighten Out Our Working Relationships—Let's Choose To Manage

Those who do the organization's work are the managers that matter most. This has always been true, though not always recognized. Our system of management has been informal—the system of Role Sets. It has been largely unconscious and nearly invisible. It is constantly present, persistently influencing everyone's behavior. It keeps our behavior stable and predictable so that cooperation can happen. But it can also cause behavioral change to be both physically and emotionally dangerous. For an organization to be flexible and responsive to opportunities and threats, we must all become better role senders and receivers.

To change our performance or someone else's, we must deal with Role Sets. Changing behavior in an organization always involves *sets* of people, never an individual alone. Everything in this book aims at helping us get our Role Set relationships right (usually we call them our *working relationships*), because this is the essence of managing ourselves and one another.

Fundamentally, this book is about human communications at work. Instead of discussing *how to communicate*; it focuses on *what to communicate*. As long as we can talk, smile, frown and point, we have most of the tools we need to deliver our messages. The problem is that many of our messages aren't about the most relevant issues. If we're going to solve the management problems of low productivity and distress at work, we must become more precise and focused in the ways we think and talk together about our work.

Taking Control with Breakthrough Systems

• • • •

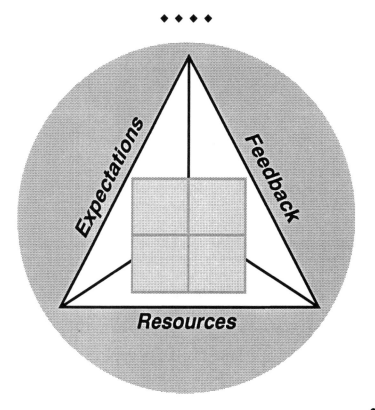

Expectations

Feedback

Resources

Overview

One of the most important concepts in management is the *Breakthrough System*. When we understand this type of system, we can remove the most important obstacles to high performance and take another step toward improving the ways we manage work. The Breakthrough System is one in which we can quickly identify and acquire all the things that we need to sustain high performance:

◆ clear information about the concrete results expected from our work;

◆ immediate and reliable feedback about how our actual performance compares to the stated expectations; and

◆ control of all the resources necessary for us to meet those expectations.

Fundamentally, this chapter is about gaining power over our own work lives. Although the term *empowerment* is bandied about a lot these days, it doesn't just refer to being happy—particularly not in the context of work. Empowerment shows in behavior, in a person's *ability to accomplish intended results.* When empowerment is defined in this way, it's possible to be very specific about the conditions that create it. Certain kinds of information and well-defined rights (authority) are required. When such conditions exist, we do our work consistently well. Without such conditions, we struggle at lower levels of effectiveness.

Being empowered at work—being able to accomplish intended results—usually leads us to see ourselves as competent and valuable people. This, in turn, often leads us to feel more confident in ourselves and more willing to participate actively in influencing all the conditions that affect our lives—at work and elsewhere. Thus, managing ourselves effectively at work—and being empowered there—benefits our lives and our society in more general ways. Although that is very good, it should be understood as a positive side effect of good management, not the direct mission of the organizations where we work.

Our mission at work is to deliver concrete products or services to customers. This very specific function establishes the basis and sets the limits for our working relationships. Only as we focus our attention on the concrete and specific results we must deliver to our customers and secure the conditions of the Breakthrough System, can we experience empowerment at work. At work, the question is always and simply: "Do we have what it takes to get our work done?"

Key Concepts

Breakthrough Systems empower us to sustain high-level performance.

◆ If we have the following conditions when doing a task, a Breakthrough System exists:

  – A clear understanding of the results expected from our work

  – Immediate and valid feedback about how our current results compare with the expected results

  – Control of all the resources needed to meet the expectations

Possible Activities

◆ Evaluate five case studies.

◆ Identify some tasks we already do with Breakthrough Systems.

◆ Identify some tasks where we can easily create Breakthrough Systems.

The Breakthrough System and Its Three Elements

We use the term Breakthrough System because something dramatic happens to any part of a performance that occurs under these conditions. If we have been performing without these conditions and then get them, our productivity leaps quickly to a much higher level. With these conditions, it is possible for us to work *smarter* instead of *harder*.

Equally important: the conditions of a Breakthrough System provide the information and authority we need to make further dramatic improvements.

A series of studies undertaken over the past 20 years indicate that most of us only realize about 50 percent of the potential productivity in resources we already have. By putting tasks into a

After the First Breakthrough

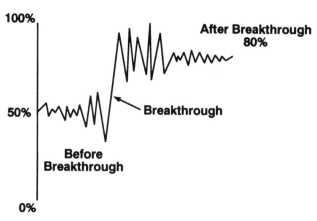

After the first Breakthrough in performance, productivity jumps
as much as 30 percent. The Breakthrough is usually followed by
a series of fluctuations, as people and systems adapt to the
new level of performance. Productivity then stabilizes at a
much higher level than before.

Breakthrough System, we can take the same materials, equipment
and skills, and produce at least 30 percent more "outputs"—products, services or other intended results. We can reach this new level
of productivity in fewer than six weeks and can sustain it indefi-
nitely—as long as we keep the Breakthrough conditions in place.

The improvements we achieve are not just in the *quantity* of
outputs—the quality is always better, too. When we have clear
expectations and reliable feedback, we don't tolerate producing 30
percent more junk.

Emery Air Freight and Other Cases

As we will see, the first two conditions of the Breakthrough
System—clear expectations and reliable, immediate feedback—are
the ones usually missing from our current work settings. Until these
two conditions are in place, we can't make intelligent use of the

resources we currently have. That is why it is always necessary to start a Breakthrough System by first establishing these two conditions.

It isn't always obvious that the main obstacle to increased productivity is a lack of clear expectations and reliable feedback. Most of us work very hard, and it seems impossible that we could get 30 percent more from the resources we currently control. Many of us immediately assume that such results will require major investments in new equipment and significant changes in the processes we are using. It is unwise, however, to make such investments and changes until we are sure that we are making full use of our current resources in Breakthrough Systems. As soon as we get the clear expectations and reliable, continuous feedback required, we usually find that we have been working harder than we needed to and that there are many better ways to use what we already have.

Emery Air Freight provides an excellent example of a Breakthrough System. When that company put Breakthrough conditions into place, the results were so dramatic that they led to a whole series of applications in many different industries.

The Emery Air Freight Story

In 1970, Emery's productivity specialist, Edward J. Feeney, began meeting with small groups of employees who did similar or identical tasks. He asked them to define reasonable standards for their outputs.

After the employees defined their standards, Feeney secretly monitored their performance for 30 days and found that the workers averaged about 48 percent of what they said was reasonable.

The employees were then asked to monitor their own work by using simple tally sheets. Each sheet was a chart comprised of eight or more vertical columns, and each column was divided into several horizontal rows (see example on page 32). Across the top, each column was labeled with an hour of the work shift: Hour 1, Hour 2, etc. Down the left side, each row was labeled with a specific task in the given job. (Here we refer to them as Task A, Task B, etc.) Each task row contained a series of evenly spaced slash marks to indicate the number of outputs (completed tasks) expected during the hours of that day's work shift. As employees performed the tasks, they made cross-marks on the appropriate slashes to indicate the number of tasks they had completed.

Typical Emery Air Freight Tally Sheet

	Hour 1		Hour 2		Hour 3		Hour 4		Hour 5		Hour 6		Hour 7		Hour 8	
Task A 6 per hr.	X X X	X X X	X X X	X X X	X X X	X X X	X X X	X X X	X X X	X X X	X X X	X X X	/ / /	/ / /	/ / /	/ / /
Task B 6 per hr.	X X X	X X X	X X X	X X X	X X X	/ / /	/ / /	/ / /	/ / /	/ / /	/ / /	/ / /	/ / /	/ / /	/ / /	/ / /
Task C 2 per hr.	X	X	X	X	X	X	X	X	X	X	X	X	X	X	/	/
Task D 1 per hr.	X		X		X		X		/		/		/		/	

Emery employees created Breakthrough Systems by using tally sheets like the one above. The blank tally marks indicate what the employees themselves defined as a reasonable daily standard. The employees then mark each completed task as they do the work. Supervisors check the sheets twice per day. In this example, the supervisor has indicated with a vertical line that he or she checked at the end of the fourth hour.

Twice per day at random times, supervisors checked to see that employees were tracking their own work. Each time the supervisors visited, they drew lines down the appropriate hour columns to indicate that they had been there. (In the illustration, one of these lines appears just at the end of the fourth hour.) The supervisors then complimented the employees on any performances that the chart indicated were on schedule or ahead of schedule. In the illustration, the employee would have been complimented on the performance of Tasks A, C and D, all of which the chart shows are at or above standard. The supervisors made no comment of any kind about task performances that were not up to standard. Thus, in the illustration, no comment would have been made about Task B. (The supervisors were following the Rules for Encouragement, which we will explore in Chapter 9.)

Forty-eight hours after Emery started this Breakthrough System, employees were averaging 94 percent of the standard they had defined. Within weeks, they were exceeding the standard. In the few months remaining of that first year, Emery was able to show a $1.5 million increase in profitability!

Three years later, when the Emery case was published, Breakthrough Systems were still in place, and the employees had made three major increases in their level of performance. Many other organizations began experimenting with the same methods.

Notice that the effort began by focusing on the first two Breakthrough conditions—clear expectations and immediate feedback. Once this information was in the hands of the people doing the work, they were able to make much better use of the resources already at hand. During the years that followed, Emery made many other improvements by adding resources and changing processes. The organization was launched on a learning curve that continues to this day.

Two other equally important elements in this success story are the *effective use of group intelligence* (e.g., the employee group's definition of a reasonable standard for their work) and the *emphasis on personal, positive feedback from supervisors.* The Breakthroughs were not accomplished by individuals working alone; they were an effect of people working together. Employees at all levels created a new set of expectations that operated in all their Role Sets.

Emery's story is just one example of how Breakthrough Systems actually look and work. Not every task we perform will require group work to set expectations, tally sheets for feedback or supervision twice a day. The Emery case is an excellent place to begin our exploration of Breakthrough Systems, but this book explores many additional methods for achieving Breakthroughs. Some of them are more appropriate for other kinds of tasks and work situations such as Projects and Troubleshooting.

Because specific Breakthrough methods differ according to the types of tasks we do, Chapters 4 through 6 of this book pay special attention to the various methods appropriate for each type of task. The basic principles, however, remain the same—clear expectations about outputs, immediate and reliable feedback and control of necessary resources. The results are always the same, too—dramatic and continuous increases in productivity.

Five Cases of Breakthrough Performance at Work

To test our understanding of Breakthrough Systems, we will consider five cases of people trying to perform work tasks. These cases are based on actual consulting experiences. In two of the cases, all the conditions for a Breakthrough System were present, and the tasks could be performed at excellent levels of productivity. In the other three cases, at least one Breakthrough condition was missing, and the result was low productivity, confusion and distress.

Determine which Breakthrough conditions are present in each case. If you think the Breakthrough System is complete, you will put check marks in each of the three boxes following the case.

Immediately after the boxes, we offer the answers, based on what we found in the actual situations. Compare your answers with ours, and proceed to the next case. By the end of the fifth case, you should be pretty good at identifying the three essential characteristics of a Breakthrough System.

Case 1—Dolores

Part of Dolores's job is to collect monthly utility-bill payments from customers at a service counter in her office. When doing this part of her job, Dolores is expected to complete at least 30 transactions per hour—an average of one transaction every two minutes.

For each transaction, Dolores creates a record of one kind or another, and at any moment she is able to glance at a clock and quickly count these records. Dolores's supervisor asks her to count and record the number of transactions she completes at least once per hour.

Breakthrough Conditions

☐ Dolores clearly understands the results expected for this task.

☐ Dolores knows within any two-hour period how her actual performance compares to the expected results.

☐ Dolores controls the resources necessary to meet the expectations.

Author's Answers

Expectations: Dolores clearly understands the results expected for this task. You should have a check mark in the first box.

Feedback: Dolores knows within any two-hour period how her actual performance compares to the expected results. You should have a check mark in the second box.

Resources: Dolores controls the resources necessary to meet the expectations. You should have a check mark in the third box.

Case 2—Frank

Frank authorizes credit card purchases when merchants telephone his office. He uses a computer to locate the relevant credit card account information, then determines whether the purchase amount falls within the card's limit.

The computer counts the calls that Frank and each of his coworkers answer. At the end of every month, the computer generates a printout for the supervisor, which lists the total number of calls each employee handled that month. The computer also lists the average number of calls each employee handled in an hour. The supervisor sits down at the beginning of each month to discuss this record with Frank and each of his colleagues.

Breakthrough Conditions

❑ Frank clearly understands the results expected for this task.

❑ Frank knows within any two-hour period how his actual performance compares to the expected results.

❑ Frank controls the resources necessary to meet the expectations.

Author's Answers

Expectations: Frank does not know what is expected from this task. He has the information necessary to make the required authorization decisions, but he does not know the *pace* at which he is expected to make these decisions. The hourly average for Frank and his coworkers is a floating standard—no one ever knows what it is at any given time. An acceptable pace last month may not be acceptable in the current month. Frank can't be sure. You should not have a check in the first box.

Feedback: The only performance feedback Frank gets from his supervisor is once a month. You should not have a check mark in the second box.

Resources: You should have a check mark in the third box. Whenever it is apparent that clear expectations or immediate feedback are missing, assume that the necessary resources are available. Most of the time, this assumption will turn out to be correct. If this assumption is wrong, only after expectations and feedback have been established will you know exactly what to do about the resource problems.

Postscript: When the computer program was revised to give Frank immediate feedback about how his current performance was compared to a fixed expectation, Frank met and exceeded the expectations every hour.

Case 3—Harry

Harry provides information to clients who ask questions at the counter in his office. He knows that at the end of the year his performance appraisal will include an assessment of how he deals with clients. So far, the supervisor has never said anything to him about this part of his work. Three or four times per year, Harry's employer conducts brief exit surveys to determine how customers feel about the service they received, and Harry is informed about the general results of these surveys.

Breakthrough Conditions

❏ Harry clearly understands the results expected for this task.

❏ Harry knows within any two-hour period how his actual performance compares to the expected results.

❏ Harry controls the resources necessary to meet the expectations.

Author's Answers

Expectations: Harry does not know what is expected on this task in terms of "friendliness." Since it is important enough to be a feature of his formal appraisal, friendliness should be defined. You should not have a check mark in the first box.

Postscript: Data eventually gathered in customer exit-surveys revealed that the following specific behaviors were sufficient to generate excellent satisfaction ratings: initiating eye contact within three seconds and smiling and using the client's name as soon as possible. "Small talk" actually turned out to damage the ratings—clients thought that this behavior wasted time and were irritated to hear it while they waited in line.

Feedback: Harry doesn't get any regular feedback on the "friendliness" part of his performance except his private interpretation of how clients are responding. When occasional exit surveys were implemented, however, they indicated that clients actually *felt* a lot less happy than they behaved. You should not have a check mark in this box.

Postscript: The client-survey data, plus an informal system of reminders that the employees worked out among themselves, provided the feedback necessary to improve this part of the workers' performance. The improvement then made an important contribution to the business's success.

Resources: Once the expectations were defined, even Harry—who was not a particularly happy or friendly person—was able to please the customers. You should have a check mark in the third box.

Case 4—Ed

Ed is one of three people in a department responding to customer inquiries by phone. When no customers call, the department is involved in other work. It has been made clear that someone should answer the phone before the third ring and should be as quick and courteous as possible in answering the customer's questions.

If a customer asks questions Ed can't answer, he refers the caller to one of his two coworkers or to another department. No records are kept of the calls Ed and his coworkers answer.

Breakthrough Conditions

❏ Ed clearly understands the results expected for this task.

❏ Ed knows within any two-hour period how his actual performance compares to the expected results.

❏ Ed controls the resources necessary to meet the expectations.

Author's Answers

Expectations: Neither Ed nor anyone else in his department knows precisely what is expected of their phone-answering performance. Ed's group had developed a terrible reputation among customers. None of the three workers knew when it was their turn to answer the phone, and they tended to wait each other out. The phone often rang more than three times. By the time one of the workers answered, his or her voice conveyed irritation that customers tended to take personally. You should not have a check mark in the first box.

Postscript: The employees agreed to a schedule in which they took turns answering the phone every third hour. For a while, the employees passed a large rubber ear to the team member whose turn it was to answer the phone. They practiced their phone greetings and discovered that if they forced themselves to smile while talking on the phone, they could get their voices to sound more relaxed and friendly. The employees also deliberately listened for and started using the customers' names.

Feedback: No feedback systems were in place to help the group monitor the phone-answering part of their performance. The group learned about their terrible reputation from a corrective action team in another department, which was conducting a customer-satisfaction survey. You should not have a check mark in the second box.

Postscript: Ed's team started using **Thirty-Second Reports** (See Chapter 6) to monitor themselves. In the other department's follow-up survey, Ed's group received several unsolicited compliments from customers.

Resources: It turned out that no one in Ed's group was fully competent to answer even the most commonly asked questions. They referred more than 70 percent of their callers to other people or asked customers to call back when someone with an answer would be available. You couldn't have known this, however. Since expectations and feedback were missing, you should have assumed the resources were adequate—making the resources box a "yes."

Postscript: The team held a few study sessions to teach one another the answers to the most frequently asked questions and established a network of contacts in other relevant departments.

Case 5—Anna

Anna audits client case files. She has been doing this for three years and is thoroughly familiar with all the procedures and references involved, but she uses a checklist to make sure she examines every critical detail. Anna leaves a copy of this checklist in each case file when she completes her audit. Since Anna is expected to review 15 cases per hour, she takes 30 cases at a time from the files and checks every 2 hours to see whether she is ready for the next 30.

Breakthrough Conditions

❑ Anna clearly understands the results expected for this task.

❑ Anna knows within any two-hour period how her actual performance compares to the expected results.

❑ Anna controls the resources necessary to meet the expectations.

Author's Answers

Expectations: Anna clearly understands the results expected for this task. You should have placed a check mark in the first box.

Feedback: Anna knows within any two-hour period how her actual performance compares to the expected results. You should have placed a check mark in the second box.

Resources: Anna controls the resources necessary to meet the expectations. You should have placed a check mark in the third box.

Evaluating Our Own Tasks

Now that we've examined some other people's working conditions, let's take a look at our own. It's a good idea to first look for examples in which we already have a Breakthrough System. These conditions usually exist in the parts of our work that we are currently doing very well and enjoy the most.

My Success with Breakthrough Systems

On a piece of paper, use the format below to describe one of your current successes with Breakthrough Systems.

Task:

Specific results expected from performance:

Reliable feedback, available in any two-hour period, about how my actual performance compares with the expected results:

Resources I control to meet these expectations:

Looking to our own success is always a good place to begin learning. The correlation between our own success and our current use of Breakthrough Systems clarifies that we are not suggesting something completely new or especially difficult. Instead, the use of Breakthrough Systems feels familiar and easy—no big deal. Furthermore, we may begin noticing how many different and simple methods are available to help us clarify expectations and establish immediate and reliable feedback for us.

Let's also consider some of the tasks we perform that are not yet in Breakthrough Systems. At this point, all we need to do is to name the tasks and identify what's missing. If ideas about how to correct the conditions come immediately to mind, that's great. But we will have lots of opportunities later in this book to think further about these tasks.

Empowering Ourselves for Work

To be able to do our work well, we must have the conditions of a Breakthrough System. As we work to create these conditions for ourselves and our colleagues, we empower ourselves. This is an entirely appropriate way to think about empowerment at work. No one can do anything more to empower themselves or others at work than to create Breakthrough Systems.

The "managers" in the organization aren't any more able to empower us than we are ourselves. Those of us who do the daily work know best what we can reasonably be expected to accomplish, how to create useful performance-feedback systems and which resources we need to accomplish the expected results. Managers can only get this kind of information by talking to the people who do the work. They can talk to us themselves, or they can hire others to gather the information (consultants, for example), but the source is always the people who do the work. And even when all the information has been gathered, it can't become useful until those of us who do the work understand it and choose to use it in managing ourselves.

Managers can, of course, make it easier for us to develop and maintain Breakthrough Systems. They can help us determine appropriate expectations—the pace and quality requirements that will enable us to coordinate our work with that of others and satisfy customers. Sometimes managers can help us get access to equipment and software that make feedback systems easy. They can use their authority to make sure that we have the resources we need to get our work done. Managers also can ensure that others respect our authority to control the resources we need to do our own work. When individuals perform these tasks, they are performing the role of formal management.

The role of manager is another set of tasks that an empowered person must perform. Our managers need to do their work in Breakthrough Systems, too. Their expectations should be that all those they support are working in Breakthrough Systems. Their feedback is provided by those of us they support—we tell them whether or not we are in Breakthrough Systems. When we are not in Breakthrough Systems, our managers' job is to work with us and with other managers to make sure the information and other resources are corrected.

To support us in these ways, managers must be empowered by our cooperation. We empower them to perform their roles as much as they empower us. If we wait for them to take the initiative to empower us, we unnecessarily delay the process of moving ourselves into Breakthrough Systems. We can start the process of empowerment as easily as they can. Not to do so usually leads us into some sort of victim role, the ultimate consequence of which is that others with more initiative take our customers and our jobs.

We need to remember that managers only have the power to manage if we consent to their exercise of that power. When we consent, we do so because we see managers using their formal authority to help us get into Breakthrough Systems and stay there. When we don't see managers acting in this way, we tend to withdraw our respect, our minds and our energy. We wait for them to figure out our problems (which they can't do very well by themselves). We don't do anything until we're told (and managers tell us the wrong things to do); and then we do exactly what we are told to do. In this way, we make our managers fail. Of course, we discover in the process that we have to fail first.

We can keep everybody empowered by insisting that we all get into Breakthrough Systems and by insisting that we all act in ways that maintain these conditions. Empowering ourselves and everyone else in the organization is the way to go. Our working relationships are interdependent; we succeed or fail together.

Summary: Breakthrough Systems Are Paths to Empowerment

At work, the direct path to empowerment is a set of job-focused actions that we undertake together. Actual empowerment starts happening very quickly when we talk about the results we are expected to deliver to our customers. Empowerment builds as we get immediate and reliable feedback about how we are satisfying those expectations. Empowerment results from gaining control of the resources necessary to meet those expectations.

If any one of the Breakthrough conditions is missing, we stop being powerful enough to get our work done. We can actually feel this loss of power in the fatigue we experience at the end of the work day. We go home feeling not only tired in our bodies but confused and distressed as well. Without the empowerment of Breakthrough Systems, we have to work harder both physically and emotionally.

When we have all the Breakthrough conditions, we are able to work intelligently and cooperatively—we work smart instead of hard. At the end of the day, we know what we've accomplished and have some confidence in our ability to overcome problems and take advantage of opportunities.

It has become obvious that the creation of Breakthrough Systems at work leads many of us to greater self confidence elsewhere in our lives. We learn at work about our abilities to make and honor commitments. We become more effective at working with others. We find ourselves succeeding in our jobs as individuals and as team members. Work consumes much of our time and energy, and when we succeed at work, we put a large part of our lives in order. Usually, our family and friends recognize and show approval for our success at work and for the social skills we develop in the process. Through their respect, we learn a greater respect for ourselves.

The more we experience ourselves as capable and valuable persons, the more likely we are to be assertive in other forms of social cooperation—in our families, schools, religious communities, clubs, community associations and various forms of government. Although this wider benefit is not the specific purpose of most organizations that employ us, it is a very constructive side-effect.

Work is not the whole of life. The production of products and services for customers is only one of the ways in which we contribute to our society's quality of life. In the process of making this contribution, however, we often learn the skills and gain the self confidence that help us enrich our lives in many additional forms of social cooperation. We should desire this for each other and rejoice as we see it happening. But let us remember that the most direct contribution our working relationships can make to such personal development is to make sure we succeed in our work. Success at work comes from managing ourselves and each other in Breakthrough Systems.

Making Tasks
Meaningful

◆ ◆ ◆ ◆

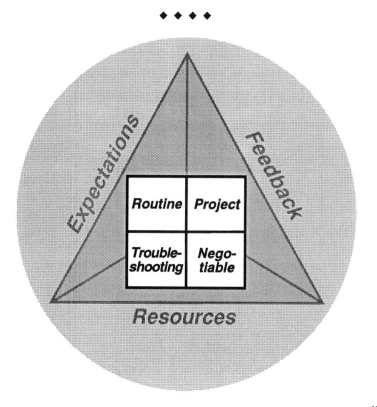

Overview

It is not always easy to identify the outputs at the center of our working relationships. To help, this chapter introduces two more important management concepts: the *Basic Systems Model* and the *Task Grid*.

The Basic Systems Model describes how all the parts of a task performance are supposed to fit together and helps identify which parts are failing or missing. The model says all tasks are alike in that they have six elements: *inputs, process, outputs, customers, pace feedback* and *quality feedback*.

The Task Grid, on the other hand, is a convenient way of noticing how the tasks that make up each role differ from one another. The Task Grid identifies four types of tasks: *Routine, Project, Troubleshooting* and *Negotiable*. Each of these task types requires different methods for clarifying expectations, establishing appropriate feedback methods and gaining control of the necessary resources. We must recognize and understand these differences so that we can select appropriate methods for putting tasks into Breakthrough Systems.

Using these concepts also helps us deal with questions about our motivation to work. Often the source of low motivation at work is our more-or-less conscious resentment about having to spend our lives on something that seems meaningless. In examining our own motivation, we must consider the *relationship* between our outputs and our customers—the ways that customers *use* our outputs. Then we can ask ourselves: Is that worth the time and talent that I invest at work? If we don't like what our customers do with our outputs, we're in the wrong work. In the long run, we do ourselves and our organizations harm unless we can leave work every day saying to ourselves, "I have delivered products and services to customers who have used them to do things I consider good and right."

Key Concepts

- ◆ All work tasks can be understood as Basic Systems with the following elements:
  - *Inputs*—the material, supplies, equipment, skills, information, authority and other resources required for performance

- *Process*—the procedures by which the inputs are manipulated and analyzed
- *Outputs*—the tangible and intangible results of the process
- *Customers*—the people or systems that receive and use the outputs
- *Pace Feedback*—information about whether the performance is occurring at the right speed;
- *Quality Feedback*—information about whether the outputs' features and performance are satisfying the customers' requirements

◆ The Task Grid divides tasks into four basic types, each of which requires different methods for developing Breakthrough Systems:
- Routine
- Projects
- Troubleshooting
- Negotiable

◆ The *purpose* of our work is found in the relationship between our outputs and our customers. We find work meaningful when we like the way customers use our outputs.

Possible Activities

◆ Identify the types of tasks that make up our role.
◆ Identify the outputs produced from the tasks we do.

Outputs: The Focus of Working Relationships

Outputs—specific products and services—lie at the center of our working relationships. Work relationships differ from other relationships because they have a specific purpose: to produce outputs for customers.

Of course, the psychological processes of all relationships are varied, complex and fascinating. They are the source of emotional stimulation. We could try to sort out our relationships in terms of these processes, but we would soon find ourselves bogged down in the complexity, uncertainty and semantic confusion characteristic of psychology. A simpler approach (and also a less precise one) is to distinguish relationships according to the function—the purpose or outputs—of these processes.

Most of us have many different types of relationships—friendships, marriage or partnership, parenting, play, work, etc.—and each relationship has a different purpose in our lives. Using this functional model, we might say that the purposes of friendship include mutual emotional support and the pursuit of shared interests. The purposes of marriage or partnership might include long-term companionship, economic advantages and/or childrearing. The purpose of a parenting relationship is to help children develop into socially functional adults. Playmates relate for the purpose of playing a sport or other game. Working relationships are those in which the purpose is to produce products or services for customers.

Breakthrough Performance uses a functional definition of relationships because it is the most common way of thinking about relationships in organizations. But it is not the only way. Like a map, this model gives us a simple, deliberately artificial way to keep all the complexities of reality in convenient categories. Just as a map is never the same as the territory it represents, so this functional model of relationships is not as complex as the actual experience of relationships. Our experience of a relationship may be a multi-layered web of memories, feelings and immediate concerns. One benefit of the functional model, however, is that it can help us to prioritize these complex memories, concerns and feelings according to how relevant they are to the purpose of the relationship. The functional model suggests that we set aside the feelings and memories that are less relevant.

In a work relationship, for example, we may not like a particular colleague, but the purpose of our relationship is not to like each other; it is to work together to produce a product or service for the customers we jointly serve. Looking at the relationship this way may help us to maintain emotional balance when the relationship becomes uncomfortable. It may also help us to find ways through the discomfort by keeping us focused on our overriding goal: giving our customers what they need. In this way, the model serves us. No model deals with the whole complexity of actual relationships, but a functional model gives us a practical, common and appropriate way to stand back and think about them.

If we define our work relationships in terms of their outputs, then we had better first define the outputs. We call them by many names—products, services, deliverables, results—because our work relationships create them in many different forms. Sometimes the output is as obvious as a microprocessor or a pair of pants. But sometimes it is less obvious. What is the output of a lawyer who is counseling a client? What is the output of a doctor answering a patient's questions about impending surgery? What is the output of an engineer who is searching professional literature for help with a physics problem? What is the output of a group of people who meet to review one another's work? In these cases, we might be able to *suggest* what the purpose of the relationship is, but we can't be very precise until we can specify the intended outputs concretely.

Basic Systems Model Showing Four Elements

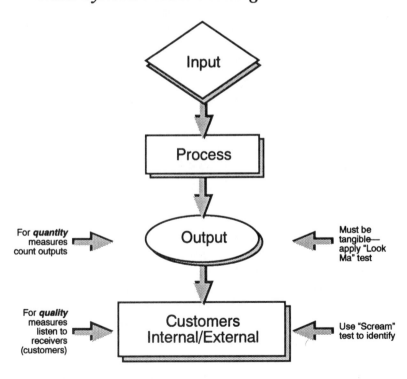

The first four elements of the Basic Systems Model

Using the Systems Model To Identify Outputs

To identify our outputs, it helps to think about our tasks as a system. As mentioned earlier, the Basic Systems Model on page 51 suggests that work tasks have six basic parts arranged in a sequential flow: *inputs, process, outputs, customers, pace feedback* and *quality feedback.*

The First Four Elements of Any System

Inputs are all the materials, supplies, equipment, skills, information, authority and other resources required by the system. Next in the sequence is the *process*—whatever is done with or to the inputs: manipulation, assembly, disassembly, testing, calculation, analysis, etc. When the process is done, the tangible (or intangible) result is an *output*—a new product, a record of service, the solution to a problem, a report, etc. The next step in the process is the *customer*, the person or system that receives the outputs and does something with them. *Pace feedback* measures whether the entire performance is occurring at the right speed; and *quality feedback* tells us if the outputs' features and performance satisfy the customers' requirements.

We will begin with a discussion of the first four elements of this system: inputs, process, outputs and customers.

Consider the task of washing and drying clothes with a relatively low-tech machine. With careful consideration, it becomes apparent that the task called "doing the laundry," is actually a super-system that includes three subsystems in sequence. The first system is washing, the second is drying and the third is folding the clothes and putting them away.

The first stage requires several inputs: dirty clothes, soap, water, a washing machine and a person to push the button. The process involves putting the clothes in the machine, adding soap and water, then turning on a motor that causes a thrashing arm inside the tub to swirl the clothes around in the soapy water, until dirt is loosened from the fabrics and dissolved in the water. Then the machine drains the dirty water, spins the water out and adds clean water for the rinse cycle. After the rinse, the machine again spins to drain water and "dry clothes." Once again, the tub is drained and the clothes are wrung out. The washing process is finished, and the output is clean wet clothes.

Dirty Clothes To Clean, Dry Clothes

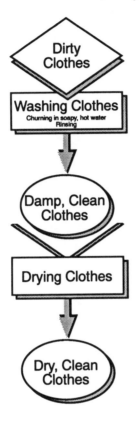

Who is the customer? At the moment, the only customer for this output is the next task or subsystem: drying the clothes.

For this second system, the inputs include clean wet clothes, a clothes dryer and a person to push the button. The process involves placing wet clothes into the dryer, selecting the temperature and turning the machine on. The output is dry clothes in a basket. And now who is the customer? Once again, the customer is the next system: folding and putting the clothes away.

For this final system, the inputs include the basket of dry clothes, storage spaces, such as shelves, drawers and closets, and the person doing the work. The process is sorting, folding and putting the clothes away. The output is clean clothes hanging or folded in their appropriate storage areas. The customers, at last, are the people who wear the clothes—and who are, of course, quick to express their delight and gratitude.

Now it's your turn. Try applying the Basic Systems Model to some other familiar tasks: making a pot of coffee, registering visitors at a reception desk, reading a book. If the system contains subsystems, identify the inputs, processes, outputs and customers for each.

Feedback Loops—Making Systems Smart

In the clothes washing system, there is only one information-handling element: the person. If we remove the person and the information the person carries from this task, nothing will get done. The other elements will lie around without any purpose to unite them or any system that will guide them toward that purpose.

Basic Systems Model

Feedback loops make a system intelligent.

Without the person, the system lacks intelligence—it cannot operate without performance expectations (standards) and performance feedback. It cannot manage any part of itself.

In this example, the worker supplies the necessary information-processing capability. The worker carries a standard in his or her head—how clean clothes look, feel and smell—and uses a sensory system to keep evaluating the clothes at all stages of the process to determine whether the standard is being met. For instance, the worker might turn off the thrasher during the washing process and pull up some wet clothes to see whether their dirty spots are gone. If so, it's time to drain the tub and move on to rinsing; if not, the person can turn the thrasher back on. This kind of information-processing is what makes the whole thing "systematic."

Before a system can be a system, it must include some information-processing capability. In the Basic Systems Model, this capability can be represented as two feedback loops. One regulates the pace at which the system moves; the other regulates the quality of the outputs.

In the preceding illustration, the pace loop is an arrow moving from the outputs back toward the inputs. The loop carries information about the number of outputs that have been produced within some specified period—e.g., one basket of clean, damp clothes every half hour. This information flows back to the beginning of the ongoing process and becomes an input to the system to help keep it on schedule.

The quality loop is an arrow that moves from the customer back to the inputs and process. This loop carries information about whether or not the customer is happy with features of the outputs. In our illustration, when interrupting the washing process to see whether the dirty spots are gone, a worker acts in place of the customer to provide feedback. Until the dirty spots are gone, there's no point in moving on to the drying process, so the worker turns the thrasher back on. The worker makes observations, compares that data to the standard for cleanliness, then feeds the results of the comparison back into the system to ensure that the process creates an output with features that will satisfy the customer.

If the spots are stubborn, the worker must do some figuring with both the quality and pace feedback: "How can I stay on schedule if I have to keep the thrasher running on these clothes?" Maybe the worker modifies the inputs or the process by adding special spot removers or sorting out the clothes with stubborn spots and running them through the washer again with the next load of clothes. The worker makes adjustments until both the pace and quality feedback loops carry information indicating that the process is meeting its standards. Now we have a complete system—one that is intelligently managed.

Notice that the feedback loops actually represent additional subsystems for information processing. The standards and the observations of current performance are inputs—which are compared—a process that occurs in the worker's brain. The comparison yields an output: a decision to maintain or change the larger system for washing the clothes. The customer for these outputs—decisions—is the larger clothes-washing system.

Through automation, we transfer some of the information-processing activity to a machine. The modern washer-dryer combination, for example, has a lot of information-processing capability already built in. After we insert the clothes and washing chemicals, we make choices on a control panel, to set standards for water temperature and cycle times. (Some of the choices are so attractive—*warm* and *gentle*—that it's hard to think of them as standards. They make you want to climb right in and take the trip yourself!)

Then we flip a switch and sit down to read while the machine does all the rest. The washer adds and tests the water temperature, times its thrashing, spins out the dirty wash water on another timed cycle, adds rinse water of the proper temperature, thrashes and spins on two more timed cycles, stops and sounds a buzzer to indicate that the clothes are washed. We move the damp, clean clothes to the dryer and set up new standards on that machine's control panel. It does the work and sounds a buzzer when it's done.

Of course, we still have to fold and sort the clothes and put them away. And there are some other things the machines don't do—such as sorting the clothes by color. So if we don't pay attention, we get an output called "weird-colored tennis socks."

"LOOK MA!"—Keeping the Focus on Outputs

Since our working relationships are all about outputs, we must be able to examine our work situations, recognize their sequences of subsystems and separate the outputs from all the other elements. Since outputs can become inputs for another system, there may be some confusion at first. But outputs are never a process—they are what is left over when a process has been completed. Nor should outputs ever be confused with customers—outputs are what we *deliver* to customers. And outputs are not the measurements flowing in the feedback loops—outputs are the concrete results being measured, evaluated and represented in the subprocess of a feedback loop.

It is especially easy to confuse outputs and the information about them that feedback loops carry. A common example is when someone says, "My output is a satisfied customer!" No. Satisfaction is a kind of information in the quality-feedback loop that flows from customers. It is desirable information, but it only comes after we have delivered some concrete product or service that provokes satisfaction. That deliverable is our output. Customer satisfaction is feedback.

We can say the same about all the measurement systems in the workplace. Our outputs are not *zero defects, profits* or *on-time delivery.* We often state our goals in terms of measurements but measurements are not our outputs. The whole point of measurements is to guide our attention back to the outputs they describe.

Confusion about outputs and their measures can be fatal to an organization. If we ignore our outputs and focus on the measurements (e.g., profit or quantity), we may tend toward fraud. We may try to "make the numbers look good" while ignoring the shabby features of our outputs. Sooner or later, our delusion or deception will be discovered and our most precious possession—a reputation for personal integrity and quality work—will be damaged. The less we are trusted, the less able we will be to gain cooperation. Others, especially our customers, will become suspicious adversaries and will find more reliable people with whom to work as quickly as they can.

As we will discuss later, confusing outputs and their measures can also have a negative effect upon our motivation. Working just for a paycheck—a measure instead of an output—usually leads us to resent the amount of time and energy we spend at work.

One way to be sure that we have identified an output is to apply the "Look, Ma!" test. If we can point to something and say, "Look, Ma! This is what I did at work today!" then it's an output. It's concrete and tangible, and two or more of us can agree that it exists. We can literally point to an output and say, "There it is." Both of us may not understand what we are looking at, but we will be able to agree that something is physically there for us to see.

But how do we pass the "Look, Ma!" test if a substantial part of our work is thinking, giving verbal advice or decision making? Attorneys, teachers, scientists, engineers, doctors, consultants, staff experts—a lot of professionals—are in this category. In these systems of work, the inputs include our education, various databases that we use and the specific variables of unique problems that we try to solve. Our processes include *analysis, cognitive modeling, evaluation* and prescription. Often, what we give our customers is a discussion and perhaps some advice. That's what they want, and when we do it well, our customers are satisfied and keep coming back for more. In such cases, what output can we show Ma?

We can't point to the advice. If Ma came to watch, all she would see is our process of reading, working at a computer or talking. At her next social function, when others ask her, "What does your child do?" she would have to say, "Well, she has a job in the legal department, but I don't really know what she does there."

Who cares if ordinary people can't see the tangible results of what professionals do all day at work? We should all care! People tend to distrust what they don't understand. And these days, people in our society don't have much confidence in the individuals and organizations that do this kind of work. The reputations of lawyers, politicians, doctors, scientists, executives, engineers, teachers, consultants, psychologists, clergy, social workers, planners, police officers, computer experts, software designers and service representatives aren't very good. Shareholders, taxpayers and clients don't seem to know what they are getting for their money. All too often, there is no tangible output that they can identify ahead of time, or none that they can use to determine whether these professionals have done any work at all or done it well. These customers are not inclined to invest capital, pay taxes, allocate budgets or fund the paychecks of people they aren't sure are working.

"Show me what you've done" is, in fact, a demand that we all make upon one another. Our ability to point to our outputs is actually a requirement for sustaining a reputation for trustworthiness and reliability. Those of us whose work is full of intangibles are especially obligated to create and identify visible results for our work. Our outputs really are reports, case files, time logs, designs, test results, lists of documents searched and people interviewed, graphs, course outlines, books and articles, accessible databases, lines of computer code, computer screens full of menus and information, machines operating under the control of our software. These tangibles are what prove that we have been at work. We don't recognize Albert Einstein's value as a mathematician until we see the formula $E = mc^2$.

What others see is what we get by way of their understanding and respect. And until we focus on outputs, we usually can't maintain our own self-respect as members of the work force.

To Think Systematically, Think Backward

One more point about outputs needs emphasis at this stage of our discussion: outputs are the *starting point* of any analysis of a work system. Don't start trying to figure out a system by looking at its inputs—always begin at the end and move *backwards* through the Basic Systems Model. No matter how complex the system or combination of systems, to analyze it systematically you must mentally reach in and grab hold of the outputs first. As you pull on these concrete things, the rest of the analysis will follow along in its proper order.

Next, identify customers. Then see what information—if any— is in the feedback loops. This information tells whether the system is moving fast enough and whether it's producing outputs that satisfy customers. Until we have examined our outputs, customers and the pace and quality feedback, we can't know why we are bothering to examine the process or inputs.

If everyone is happy with the pace and quality of outputs, examining the process isn't a very high priority at all. Only after we discover that something is wrong with the pace or quality can we intelligently examine the process and inputs. When we understand the output, we can ask specific questions: "Why is this system producing this particular defect?" Then we can begin solving the problem efficiently.

Using the Task Grid To Define and Separate Tasks

We have said that the Basic Systems Model can be applied to all work tasks. The Model's six elements—inputs, process, outputs, customers, pace and quality feedback—are characteristic of all tasks. But when it comes to putting various tasks into Breakthrough Systems, the methods we use will differ—no single combination of expectations, feedback and resources is appropriate for every task we do. Before we can effectively clarify reasonable expectations with our Role Sets, we must think systematically about each of the tasks that make up our role, and recognize their differences and similarities.

The task of running silicon wafers through a computer-chip fabrication process is very different from constructing the building in which that process occurs. Producing phone bills is very different from using a phone to answer customers' complaints about their bills. Restoring a computer system that has crashed because of mechanical or software failures is quite different from using a computer to analyze costs for a new product idea. But the task of running wafers is, in some ways, like the task of producing phone bills. Dealing with customer complaints is somewhat similar to doing emergency maintenance on a computer system. These tasks are similar in type, and the Task Grid on page 61 is a helpful model for sorting tasks into four basic types—Routine, Project, Trouble-shooting and Negotiable.

Building the Task Grid—Predictability and Delay Tolerance

Notice that these four task types are arranged on vertical and horizontal axes labeled *predictability* and *delay tolerance* respectively. What distinguishes each type of task from the others is the degree to which it can be predicted ahead of time and the degree to which it can be postponed.

A task is predictable when we are thoroughly familiar with it and know everything about its Basic System before we begin—its inputs, process, pace and the quality of outputs that will satisfy our customers' needs. The less we know about the elements of a task's Basic System, the less predictable the task will be.

A task's delay tolerance is the extent to which it must be done exactly on schedule.

Task Grid

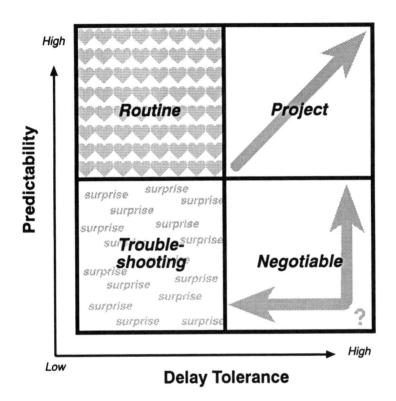

The Task Grid is a helpful model that separates work tasks into four basic types.

The Four Types of Tasks—Routine, Project, Trouble-shooting and Negotiable

A *Routine task* is not necessarily one that we do frequently; it's a task in which the elements and steps are predictable and cannot be delayed. The steps of a high-speed manufacturing process are routine.

The task of processing silicon wafers into computer chips is a good example. The manufacturing process can be perfected because we can predict with great precision the inputs that are required, the exact procedures we must follow and the pace and the reliability that our customers will require. Elaborate subsystems can be established to monitor pace and quality and ensure that we have adequate feedback to control the process at every step. The delay tolerance is zero, because if any one of the subtasks falls off-pace, the whole line may crash, leaving all kinds of materials wasted in various stages of incompletion. To keep the line moving, every task in the sequence must occur exactly when scheduled.

The task of producing semi-monthly paychecks is similarly routine. The task is predictable, and chaos is likely to erupt if the outputs are not delivered to customers on time.

With a *Troubleshooting task*, delays are also intolerable and can sometimes be fatal. But these tasks are inherently unpredictable. Two examples are emergency repairs of machinery and paramedic rescues. The emergency specialist doesn't know when the machine or person will break down, what will cause the failure, what will have to be done to correct the problem. The first step in performing this kind of task is to go to the site of the problem and begin figuring out what needs to be done. It is an important task that someone must be prepared to do, but it is inherently unpredictable and must be handled *immediately*.

Answering customer complaints is a less dramatic but equally unpredictable Troubleshooting task. Like customers with broken machines or bodies, those with service complaints are not very tolerant about delays.

A *Project*, on the other hand, is a task in which we invent something unique or undertake a change. It usually involves relatively predictable, planned steps. A Project also can be delayed, and predictable delays can be built into the deadline schedule. If at some stage of the Project we must learn or do something unfamiliar, we estimate how long it will take to get over the learning curve. Then we build slack time into that step to ensure that the overall deadline can tolerate this delay.

A Project to design a revolutionary new computer microprocessor, for example, must be planned with delays in mind. Because new technology is being mastered, rough estimates must be made about how much time workers will need to learn the new information. Time will be added into the Project schedule to account for these uncertainties. The deadline is only reliable to the extent that appropriate delay tolerance has been built into it.

A *Negotiable task* is usually a hybrid of a Project and a Troubleshooting task. Negotiables come up unexpectedly, but can be delayed if more pressing priorities must be met first. Negotiables are nonemergency unpredictables with delay tolerance.

If we work in a marketing department, for example, we may be asked to analyze a product opportunity that no one had foreseen. We must fit this new task into our already full schedule by comparing its urgency with that of our other tasks, and perhaps by considering the availability of other experts on our team. A typical negotiating response might sound like this: "We can't start this analysis until three weeks from now, when all the necessary team members are available. Then it will take us about three weeks to complete. This is the best I can do, given my current resources. If that's not soon enough, you'll have to take your request to a higher level of decision maker."

If, however, the person requesting the analysis says, "I've just spoken to the head of marketing and she's given this top priority—you will probably get a call from her any minute. We are to start this today, and our deadline is this coming Thursday." Now the Negotiable task has become a Troubleshooting one—it is a priority that cannot be delayed.

The Task Grid can classify systems roughly at the macro level, but once we begin examining the task's subsystems, we may find a mixture of types.

For example, when a Project begins to converge—usually during the final third of its schedule—the team members often find themselves spending a lot more time dealing with surprise emergencies. At the macro level, the task is a Project. But within this larger task are Troubleshooting subsystems. The same sort of mix occurs in high-volume production, a task which is Routine at the macro level. Occasionally, team members must make emergency repairs to equipment—a Troubleshooting task.

Another example is customer service. The macro-task is essentially Troubleshooting—responding immediately to customers' unpredictable needs for information or help. But if the customer needs basic information about a bill, we can use a computer to call up the customer's records in a Routine way.

Your Turn: Analyzing Your Key Tasks

On the following worksheet, take a few minutes to list the tasks you do in the process of performing your role. Start by listing the tasks you have done during the past five days. Then test your understanding of the Task Grid by labeling each of your tasks Routine, Troubleshooting, Project or Negotiable. The following guidelines have been designed to help you.

Stick with the Definitions

Remember that a Routine task is one that is both predictable and low in delay tolerance—not a task that you "do all the time." (Some of us do Troubleshooting all the time—it's the heart of our role.)

Look for Interdependencies

Be prepared for the fact that some of your tasks are subsystems of other macro tasks on your list. Try stringing these subtasks together with arrows that show their appropriate sequence and interdependencies.

Next, List Outputs

The next step is to list the outputs for each task. At this stage of analysis, it isn't important to distinguish between good outputs and bad ones. If the output is a pair of pants, that's all you need to say— you don't need to know the stress tolerance for the seams.

Remember that an output is always a concrete reality that will pass the "Look, Ma!" test. Sometimes, a report is the only evidence that your process occurred. In such cases, the report is your output— include its name on your worksheet. An attorney's process is often to give advice by telephone, and the only evidence is a "Billable Time Report." This is what the attorney would show Ma.

Share Your Task Analysis

If you're stuck, spend a few minutes discussing your lists, flow charts and "Look, Ma!" outputs with one or two teammates. That's usually enough to get you started in this process of identifying and analyzing your tasks.

In the chapters ahead, you may find this process a helpful shortcut to clarifying the expectations and adjusting the feedback systems for your work. It can help you design your own custom-made Breakthrough Systems, and it will be immensely helpful in turning your Role Set into a support group instead of a cause of distress.

Analyzing My Key Tasks

My Tasks	Task Type*	My Outputs
1.		
2.		
3.		
4.		
5.		
6.		
7.		
8.		
9.		
10.		
11.		
12.		

*R=Routine; P=Project; T=Troubleshooting; N=Negotiable

Finding Meaning in How Customers Use Our Outputs

So far, this discussion of tasks has been very intellectual and mechanical. We've ignored more emotional questions, such as: "How do we feel about our work?" "Do we like it?" "Do we want to do it?" Fundamentally, of course, these are questions about what motivates us to do the work we do.

No consideration of work is complete without some regard for the emotional aspect of reality. And since we now have some common ways of thinking about work, especially the Basic System Model, we also have some ways of trying to make sense out of this potentially swampy inner territory.

We Choose How We Feel about Work

A discussion of motivation must begin with an understanding that our emotions are things we control. Emotions are literally what we experience as the neural and chemical control processes of our brain prepare the rest of our body to react with a previously learned pattern of behavior. Emotions are the experience of getting ready to use a habit. (The last chapters of this book address emotions in greater detail.) This process happens very rapidly and is based upon earlier experiences, evaluations and decisions. Some of us don't realize that we are choosing—it feels automatic, natural and necessary. But, in fact, all emotions and the habits that they guide have been learned and can be changed if we choose to do so.

This individual freedom of emotions is also not obvious because every society invests enormous energy in teaching us how we should feel. Society uses our Role Sets—families, schools, religious and ethnic communities, friendships and coworkers—to teach us which habitual emotional responses are acceptable. And society defines those who share a sense of acceptable emotions and habits as responsible adults.

The fact that these norms vary greatly from society to society and are taught differently indicates that emotions are learned and are largely under the control of each individual. Even within a society, certain subgroups are taught to make unique emotional responses. Doctors are taught to stop being repulsed by the sight of blood or the bizarre behavior of those who are mentally ill. Police and soldiers are taught to use their fear of violence differently than most of the rest of us. Since our emotional responses are learned, we can change our emotions by choosing to learn new ones.

No one else is responsible for how we feel about our work. No one can make us want, or not want, to work. We can blame no one else for our state of motivation.

Thus, our original question—how do we feel about our work?—should be asked differently: "How are we *choosing* to feel about our work? Do we choose to feel like working or not?"

The conditions of a Breakthrough System give us the ability—the power—to get our work done. But clear expectations, reliable and immediate feedback, and control of resources don't make us want to do the work. Even our Role Sets, with all their threats and promises, can't motivate our work performance unless we choose to feel hurt or pleased by their offerings. We can choose to ignore and even defy our Role Sets. (As we said in the first chapter, this is usually both emotionally and physically harmful, but many of us do choose to do it anyway.) Understanding our work as a system may make it easier for us to communicate and solve problems, but that understanding doesn't make us want to manage the work. Motivation, wanting to work, is a choice we make.

Enabling Customers—A Reason To Like Our Work

How do we make this choice? Choosing to work is fundamentally a choice to let our outputs represent ourselves.

We look at the outputs we know are expected—microchips, clothes, a medical diagnosis, a hamburger and fries, a report, a clean street, a ballpark—and ask ourselves how we feel about spending many hours of every day, and a huge part of our energy, bringing these specific, concrete things into existence. We can't fool ourselves about this: when all is said and done, no other evidence but these concrete outputs will bear witness to this part of our lives. Do we choose to let these things represent our lives?

Don't be shocked to find yourself saying "Frankly, I don't get real excited about a report (or a widget). I don't feel much of anything about it. It sure doesn't seem like an appropriate representation of my life." Outputs by themselves are meaningless—they just sit there. We look at them and hear our inner voices asking, "So what?"

The outputs don't become meaningful until we ask what our customers do with them. When our medical diagnosis helps make a sick person well; when the clothes we make protect people's bodies or help the wearers feel good about their appearances; when microchips make it possible for people to learn, travel safely, communicate quickly; when the hamburger nourishes a growing child's body; the relationships between outputs and customers offer a rich range of possible meanings for our work.

It should be obvious that when we consider the usefulness of our outputs and feel good about them, we are more likely to want to do our work. It's as simple, and as serious, as that.

Some of us have never considered this question. We may never have seen our customers actually use our outputs. This is a serious oversight. One of my common observations about persistent high-performers is that they spend time watching customers use their outputs. These performers almost always have a clear idea of how their outputs are being used and can quickly explain why they care about it.

The reasons people choose to care are sometimes very surprising. Consider a man who made kitty litter—sand in which pet cats poop—and showed great motivation for his work. He said, "People have to live in cities—and cities are lonely and dehumanizing without pets. There can't be healthy pets in the city without my kitty litter!"

Another person showed equal zeal for manufacturing nuclear missiles: "I want everyone to know that if anyone ever touches the red button, this thing will go exactly where it is aimed and will blow ten parts of the world into radiated dust for a thousand years. I come here every morning to guarantee it. I don't know any other way to prevent war."

These two cases illustrate very complex combinations of personal values. The workers' comments didn't emerge quickly or easily—they required serious thought and investigation.

Sometimes we can find meanings more easily, and our choices will have less unique explanations. It doesn't matter whether the explanations are difficult or unusual. The point is to think about it and to arrive at some confidence that our customers use our outputs in some way that makes our work worth doing. This is the most reliable source of motivation—seeing ourselves as part of a useful, meaningful relationship.

If we look at how customers use our outputs and like what we see, but are not wildly enthusiastic, that might be just fine. Work usually isn't the whole source of meaning in our lives and doesn't have to be. We may also have families, community involvements, recreational pursuits, quests for religious or philosophical insight—many other activities from which to draw meaning.

But we should get some sense of meaning from our work. When our work doesn't line up with our own values, then periodically—and with increasing frequency—we will find ourselves looking at the outputs and feeling a sort of disgust. Our energies literally stop flowing into our work. We must push ourselves to work harder. At the end of the day we are deeply exhausted—not just physically, but emotionally as well.

Summary: Beware of Secondary Motives for Work

Sometimes we look to secondary outputs for a source of motivation. We say to ourselves, "I don't really care about my organization's products or what customers do with them. The work is just a means to a paycheck so I can feed my kids or save enough money for retirement." Or, "I'm just here to make things more comfortable for my fellow workers; our products are not really my concern."

We should be careful about looking to secondary outputs for two reasons. First, to focus on secondary outputs makes someone else responsible for the organization's products and services. This almost always leads to socially destructive results: our organizations begin practicing morally and politically corrupt forms of competition, producing dangerous consumer products and dumping environmentally destructive wastes. Meanwhile, all the people involved excuse themselves from responsibility by saying, "I'm just doing my job." When we look to secondary sources of motivation, we take our eye "off the ball" and often allow ourselves to derive personal satisfaction at the expense of everyone else.

Second, when we try to get ourselves moving with these substitute motives, our energy doesn't flow naturally into the process and we have to work harder. This less-efficient use of our energy keeps us from realizing our full potential at work—and we may grow frustrated by seeing others excel with less effort. After a while it becomes very difficult not to resent that we are "giving up" so much of our lives to get what we say we want. We tend to be grumpy and uncooperative at work, and our resentment often spills over onto the very people and things for which we are making "the sacrifice" at work. Again, we are victims of work instead of its managers.

And it's not just our performance at work that diminishes; it's our happiness. Work usually involves some suffering, but when the suffering seems meaningless, it is truly unbearable.

If we don't feel that the ways our customers use our outputs are worth the effort we expend to create them, we must take that situation seriously. The more time we spend in such work, the more likely we are to reach a point where we don't respect ourselves and don't feel worthwhile to others. This will be our own judgment, and we will not be able to escape it without destroying the judge. That leads many of us to self-destructive behavior, so we can avoid thinking about this painful reality. It would be better to face the reality and say to ourselves, "I don't see that these outputs are worth the energy it takes me to create them." Then, make a choice to stop and accept the consequences—get another job! Having done this thinking, we'll know better what to look for.

When our work does seem meaningful, we find the energy and desire to do it, and to keep paying attention—especially to our Role Set relationships. These relationships never will be perfect, but we can make them work for our common goal—the outputs. Our sense of meaning also makes it worthwhile to risk insisting on the conditions of Breakthrough Performance: clear and realistic expectations, reliable and immediate performance feedback and control over the necessary resources.

When we have a reliable internal source of energy and motivation, we choose to accept and use our power to get the outputs delivered reliably for our customers. No longer victims, we are managers.

Section

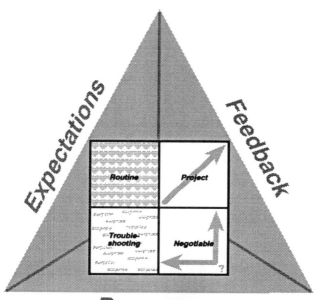

Creating Breakthrough Systems

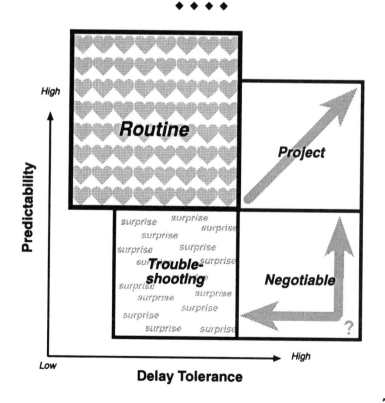

Breaking Through to Perfection with Routine Tasks

◆ ◆ ◆ ◆

Overview

In the three chapters of Section One, we got the basics in order: the vital few people we relate to through Role Sets, the essential parts of the Breakthrough System and an analysis of our tasks and outputs. We also examined how these analytic activities relate to our ability to exercise personal power and find motivation for our work.

In Section Two, we will get very specific about how to design and use Breakthrough Systems for the four types of tasks described in the Task Grid. As we develop Breakthrough Systems for these tasks, we take charge of our own performance as individuals and as teams. As we clarify expectations, get consistent and reliable feedback about our actual performance and gain control of the resources necessary to accomplish our work, we will be better able to maintain our Role Set relationships.

This chapter describes methods for developing various types of Breakthrough Systems, focusing on Routine tasks. The other two chapters in this Section will focus on Projects and the Unpredictables—Troubleshooting and Negotiables.

We begin with Routine tasks for two reasons. First, Routine tasks almost always lie at the heart of an organization's mission. Because these tasks are predictable, we can do them most reliably and efficiently. Our ability to do an organization's Routine tasks determines the organization's ability to serve its customers with reliable products and services. Routine tasks are the way that most organizations earn their right to survive.

Secondly, it is easy to create Breakthrough Systems for Routine tasks. We are familiar with these tasks, so we can easily get the information we need to clarify expectations and establish self-monitored feedback systems. Once we are empowered with that information, we are able to identify resource problems and gain control of what we need to meet the expectations. And because the outputs of Routine tasks are easiest to measure, we can see dramatic improvements in results as soon as we add the elements of Breakthrough Systems to any task where they have been missing. These improvements build confidence in our understanding of the Breakthrough System and in its effectiveness. This confidence will motivate us to create such systems for the other kinds of tasks we do.

Key Concepts

♦ Expectations for the results of Routine Tasks should include the following elements:

- The number of outputs that are required;
- The rate at which the outputs should be produced;
- How complete each output must be; and
- How precise each output must be.

♦ We can get feedback about our performance of Routine tasks via many informal tracking systems, such as: batching outputs, tally sheets or checklists.

Possible Activities

♦ Identify at least one Routine task that we already do with a Breakthrough System.

♦ Set expectations for another Routine task in which we are not yet using a Breakthrough System.

♦ Design a performance-feedback system for that same Routine task.

♦ Begin using the Breakthrough System we developed.

Setting Expectations for Routine Tasks

Routine tasks are the most important jobs for any organization. They tend to be repetitive—the sort of work we do in assembly-line fashion. Because we know so much about these tasks, our customers expect us to do them quickly and well. We usually batch them together and do as many as we can, as fast as we can.

Because we can control these tasks fairly easily, we can perfect their processes and produce outputs in volumes that make the cost per output low. In private enterprise, that's the kind of work that leads to happy customers and profits. In public administration, it's the kind of work that taxpayers depend upon most.

In fact, we could say that the basic charter of every organization is to take some set of tasks and "Routinize" them—control them so the outputs become convenient and reliable.

Reputations at Stake

As individual contributors, the Routine tasks in our roles offer the best opportunities for developing reputations for reliability and trustworthiness.

No matter how creative, analytically brilliant or personally wise we are, others in the organization—especially our Role Sets—will see us as "flakes" if we don't fill out our time sheets and expense reports on time; if we don't arrive at work or meetings promptly; if we keep forgetting appointments; if we never read our mail or return our phone calls; or if we turn our reports in late.

Coworkers may like or need us enough to tolerate our irritable traits, but they exact a price by nibbling away at our reputations— they call us sloppy, careless, childish, arrogant, unreliable. With this sort of reputation, our careers usually take a direct path away from the organization's most vital concerns. Those with reputations for reliability, on the other hand, almost always get the best new opportunities and the positions of leadership.

Our happiness and success at work depend in part upon our mastery of the Routine tasks in our role. This mastery becomes the foundation for the rest of our performance.

Fortunately, these important and well-known tasks are the easiest to get under control; people have been inventing methods for a long time. Efficiency experts call this *Scientific Management*, and they've been at it for more than 100 years. Waves of office automation over the past three decades have further advanced our ability to master the Routine tasks at the center of our day-to-day work. We have abundant resources for getting ourselves into Breakthrough Systems.

Setting Standards for Pace and Quality

As Chapter 3 explained, Routine tasks are highly predictable and have a low delay tolerance. Before we begin a Routine task, we need to know:

◆ Inputs—Required resources

◆ Process—Procedure to perform

◆ Outputs—Tangible results of the process

◆ Customers—Those who will receive our outputs and how they will receive them

Checklists and guidelines on the following pages have been designed to help us set expectations for our key Routine tasks. When we finish this step, we will be well on our way to achieving Breakthrough Performance on our jobs.

Note: Setting expectations for our own performance is not the same as creating a mission statement for ourselves or even for our team. Setting performance expectations means describing in specific terms the results that we expect from ourselves and are willing to have others expect from us—the standards that we intend to meet and that we can monitor and verify ourselves.

First, we must identify the tangible output required from each performance of the task. The output must pass the "Look, Ma!" test discussed in Chapter 3. Once we've identified the output, we describe the features of a good one. The description must have four elements: two concerning *pace* and two concerning *quality*. The two elements of pace are *quantity* and *timeliness:*

◆ the number of outputs required; and

◆ the rate at which they should be produced.

The two elements of quality are *completeness* and *accuracy:*

◆ how thoroughly each output must be done; and

◆ how precise it must be.

Examples of Pace

◆ Two cases of catsup per minute
◆ One page of finished copy per hour
◆ One customer response every five minutes
◆ Twenty phone calls initiated per hour
◆ One car washed every 90 seconds
◆ One weekly expense report every Monday by 10 a.m.

Examples of Quality

◆ A case of catsup contains 24 bottles capped, sealed and inverted.

◆ One page of copy contains 300 words correctly spelled and punctuated in grammatically correct sentences and logically organized paragraphs.

◆ Customers are given enough data from computer menus 1 through 5 that they don't need to call back with follow-up questions during the 24 hours following the call.

◆ The phone salesperson waits seven rings for someone to answer the phone or leaves a message with a person or answering machine and makes at least one appointment per hour.

◆ Soap and rinse auto body and tires and wipe or blow dry so that no dirt or streaks are visible.

◆ Fill every relevant blank in the form with appropriate text, numbers or checkmarks; back all numbers by receipts; and assure that all calculations are accurate.

The more specifically we address the issues of quantity, timeliness, completeness and accuracy, the more we can help people understand exactly what we intend to do.

In some cases, the list of quality requirements may be long—a whole book of specifications. To simplify the statement about each output's completeness and accuracy, we may refer to this set of specifications. Such an abbreviated description still indicates that we know the expectations and can verify whether our outputs meet them. For example:

◆ Produce 200 wing nuts per minute (specification W1/8-G2307).

◆ Qualify six clients per day, and provide the verified information required on form SSF1195 (attach supporting documents).

No matter how we describe the pace and quality of our expected outputs, we must be able to monitor and verify those qualities ourselves, while we are performing the task. It would be pointless, of course, to agree to meet specifications that we don't understand. And if we can't verify whether our outputs are good, we can't take corrective action—and we won't be able to get this task into a Breakthrough System.

Some aspects of our outputs' quality might be beyond our perception, however, and to that extent, these aspects are beyond our control.

For example: The width of a sub-micron etching that a machine makes on a silicon wafer to produce a computer microprocessor can only be verified with a high-powered microscope. If a problem occurs in the etching, it usually has to do with complex interactions of chemistry and physics, which the machines are supposed to control. The machine operator might not know that a problem exists; only a well-trained engineer can diagnose and correct it.

In such cases, all the operator can realistically commit to is running the machine according to the "recipe"—the process specifications for each boatload of silicon wafers. What the operator can monitor in this case is whether the machine operated as specified. The output expectation would be specified like so: "One boatload of silicon wafers every 2.5 hours machined according to the appropriate process specifications."

Testing Your Understanding

Below are some ambiguous statements about expected performance for Routine tasks. Only one of the seven statements addresses all the necessary issues. Can you identify which statement is complete, and what is wrong with the other six? Remember that each statement is supposed to describe an output by dealing with the four issues of quantity, timeliness, completeness and accuracy.

1. Write as many pages as I can in three hours every morning.
2. Write three pages per day, as quickly as I can.
3. Load and unload my two machines three times per shift.
4. Satisfy all customers who come to my teller window every day.
5. Do my work so that the quality inspector will be happy.
6. Every 30 minutes, stuff 150 labeled envelopes with a letter and all the required enclosures.
7. Draw and verify 10 circuits per week.

Answers can be found in the Appendix at the end of this chapter.

Making Sure the Expectations Are Realistic

Knowing that the expectations statement must address the four issues of quantity, time frame, accuracy and completeness does not tell us what these measures should be in any specific case. How do we determine what results are appropriate to expect from any specific task?

To answer this question, we must collect data about our current performance. This is called *baselining*, which involves establishing a baseline against which to compare future performance. With this information, we can at least set an expectation to maintain our current performance.

But we usually go beyond maintenance and set expectations for improvement. We may express these expectations as a percentage of improvement or as a trend toward perfection. Or, we may go into other organizations and compare our current performance with theirs. This practice, called *benchmarking*, is becoming quite common. Benchmarking permits us to determine what is possible and perhaps necessary if we are to compete successfully.

Ten Ways To Collect Data on Current Performance

There are many ways to get information about our current performance and that of our team and/or department. Here are ten possibilities:

1. Analyze data from Management Information Systems.
   - Ask the manager or technical resource person to get information and records about the group's:
     - input and output quantities; and
     - quality problems.

2. Sample records.
   - Select 20-50 case files at random, and check them for actions taken, in order to:
     - determine the average number of steps in the process; and
     - discover typical errors and omissions.

3. Review procedures.
   - Examine policy and procedures manuals to identify prescribed methods and to find:
     - omissions or errors causing quality problems; and
     - ways to streamline procedures or avoid overlaps.

4. Review and/or audit complaints.
   - Keep or find records of complaints from customers, auditors or quality inspectors, to find typical:

- problems in output quality; and
- errors or omissions.

5. Interview employees.
   - Regularly ask our peers to talk individually about problems they see in the processes they do, to find:
     - typical bottlenecks and overlaps in processes;
     - ways to streamline processes; and
     - individual skill development needs.

6. Form an employee task force.
   - Ask a group of peers to think together about problems they encounter in the processes they do, to find:
     - typical bottlenecks and overlaps;
     - coordination problems; and
     - common resource needs.

   Note: See Chapter 8 for information about how to charter an effective task force.

7. Count employee transactions.
   - Ask workers to keep simple tallies of each step in a process that they do every day. Count and compare to find the average number of steps for each output.

8. Set up short-interval timed laps.
   - Distribute batches of a Routine task in even lots of 10, and ask each performer to report when finished, and/or check every 30 minutes to see how many are done. Keep records to:
     - determine the average time required to complete each item; and
     - find individuals who are having problems that slow them down.

9. Make trial runs.
   - Set up a test in which three or four performers handle the same set of inputs, and time them as they complete the process. Calculate their average time, to find out how much time each output should take to create.

10. Trace inputs.

- Select a few inputs before they are processed, then recheck when the inputs have become outputs, then check the process, to:
  - determine the average number of steps in the process; and
  - discover typical errors or omissions.

Designing Self-Monitored Feedback Systems

The second key to creating Breakthrough Performance is a performance-feedback system. Once we've made clear statements about the outputs we expect from our own performance, we can start monitoring ourselves to see how we're doing. Because this feedback relates directly to our own performance, it can cause us to maintain or change our behavior. Most of the information floating around the organization never has this kind of effect. Whatever it is, it isn't performance feedback.

Turning Information into Performance Feedback

For information to be useful as performance feedback, it must be *comparative* and *available when needed.*

- ◆ It must compare our current performance with the expected standard.
- ◆ It must be available when we can use it to guide our performance toward desirable results.

No matter how much information we have about the process we are using or the concrete outputs we are creating, we can't determine how well we are doing without a standard to compare against.

Also, the more immediately available these comparative data are, the more they will affect our behavior. Such data don't usually affect our behavior unless we are getting them at least every two hours on the job. For most Routine tasks, as we will see, it is possible to create simple, informal feedback systems that are actually continuous.

Most of us naturally create performance standards for ourselves, because we like being able to evaluate whether our own work is "good." Often we ask someone we respect what they like about our outputs and then try to incorporate those features into our future outputs. Or we watch the pace of the people working next to us, and decide that we're doing all right because we're going just as fast. Or we figure that if no one is yelling at us, we must be doing okay.

But these informal standards aren't always very consistent or reliable indicators. Police officers are a good example of this point. Patrol officers keep track of their activity in 10-minute increments—a continuous log. They never have any trouble telling us *what* they have done in a given period. But if we ask, "Was that a good day's work?" we'll get some funny answers. The usual reply is one that even they don't find very satisfactory: "If the sergeant doesn't complain about it, I'm doing okay."

When we probe further to learn what the officers must do to keep the sergeant from yelling, we find that they've set up all kinds of informal standards for themselves. Formal quotas for traffic tickets are usually forbidden, for example, but informally they are very much in use by the officers who get the best ratings. Some officers invent checklists of items that they think will make their incident reports more acceptable.

The situation for patrol officers is somewhat unusual, because they have a continuous record of their actual performance. It's the *standards* that they aren't very sure about. Patrol officers suffer from a lot of Role Ambiguity (see Chapter 1 for further discussion of this concept)—not much is being done to clarify expectations for them. So the officers create their own standards and pass them along informally when they think they've got something figured out.

Most workers face the opposite problem: they have standards to meet, but no immediate and reliable way of knowing what they've actually done. Generally, people rely on their memories for this information, but memory is unreliable. At Emery Air Freight, for example, (See story in Chapter 2) people generally appeared to remember doing about twice as much as they actually had done. This is the case most of the time. No one seems to be deliberately distorting data, it's just a feature of how we remember our work. We seem to forget how much time we lost on small distractions.

People usually feel rather uncomfortable when they discover that their actual productivity is substantially less than they thought it was. And people respond differently, which can lead to unpleasant conflicts within the work team. Some feel guilty and ashamed; some fear the discovery will be made public and they'll be humiliated or punished; some feel obliged to find others to blame; some take action and create systems that help generate reliable feedback.

Discomfort is inevitable when we start keeping records of our own performance. For all the reasons mentioned, and more, it's not a very exciting prospect. We can find plenty of excuses not to evaluate our performance or to give up shortly after we've begun.

But these discomforts are unavoidable if we want to begin the process of managing ourselves more effectively. The good news is that the situation improves—the feedback ultimately helps our productivity leap to higher levels. Knowing that we are making these improvements rebuilds confidence, mutual respect with co-workers and ambition to do even better.

Tracking Ongoing Performance

Three excellent systems for tracking the outputs of Routine tasks are: *batching, tally sheets* and *checklists.* Following are explanations and examples of each method. While reading, let's think how we might use these methods to track one or two of our most important Routine tasks.

Batching

Batching means organizing our inputs or outputs so that we can glance at them at any point and determine how many we have done. A second glance at the clock will tell us whether we are on pace. We can sample our outputs every half hour to make sure that we haven't strayed from the quality requirements.

The beauty of batching is that it doesn't require any additional forms or paperwork. We usually move inputs and outputs around anyway, so we just have to move them a little differently for their arrangement to convey feedback about quantity.

Examples

- ◆ Arrange incoming components in batches of 5 or 10.
- ◆ Stack cases of inputs or outputs in groups of 20.
- ◆ Insert a marker into a stack of envelopes after every 10.

◆ Place case files in an "Out" box in groups of 5.

◆ Load a different section of the shelf or trolley each hour.

Tally Sheets

Each time we complete a Routine task, we'll make a mark of some kind.

The tally sheet developed at Emery Air Freight is an excellent example. (See page 32.) The form shows the expected number of tasks to be completed every hour—no memory work about the standard is necessary, because it is apparent on the form.

Workers make cross-marks on the pre-printed slashes every time they complete an output. To determine how current performance compares with the standard, all the workers must do is glance at the form and the clock any time during the shift.

Short-Interval Tally

We can also use a tally sheet to track short-term performances of a single Routine task (or set of tasks). A bank used the sample below to help tellers track their pace in 15- or 30-minute segments while they completed transactions at the customer windows.

Sample Tally Sheet

Time in:_____	Time out:_____	
Start:	15 minutes	30 minutes
Done:	/ / / / / / / /	/ / / / / / / /
Extra:	/ / / /	/ / / /

Note: Mark off the number completed. The standard is one every two minutes.

Innovations Abound

The variety of tally methods for longer intervals (e.g., a week or a month) seems endless. Some people use wall charts with post-it notes or colored dots, magnetic boards—even dart boards—to record the number of outputs they deliver from their Routine work. All these methods make very colorful feedback systems.

Salespeople have invented some very novel systems. One uses a wall chart depicting a large Ferris wheel. Names of customers are shown waiting in line to board the wheel (contracts under negotiation), riding the wheel (contracts on which work is being done), getting off (satisfied customers ready to go again or to make referrals), or falling off (contracts were broken or not satisfactorily completed).

Another salesperson uses a similar system, in which customers are represented as points in an oil field. Some are undergoing exploratory drilling, some are gushing, some are capped, some are dry holes. A successful system for tracking telemarketing results is shown.

Tracking Phone Calls

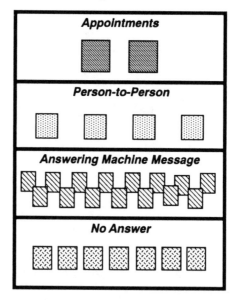

A four-part wall chart with Post-Its tracking phone calls.

Using Computers

People who work on computer terminals (e.g., providing customer service by phone) have a great opportunity to get the computer to display their tally sheets. A small window in a corner of the screen can continuously display current status. The information can be presented in more enjoyable and interesting ways than straight numbers or bar charts.

Examples

◆ Animated row-boat races in which each performance is a stroke of the oars

◆ Piggy banks filling with coins

◆ Card games in which every performance equals a card drawn in a poker hand, and prizes are awarded every 30 minutes or hour

The possibilities are endless, and Routine work can become as engaging as a video game.

Checklists

The possibilities for checklists also abound. Especially spectacular results are reported by gardeners, housekeepers and order-fulfillers.

Examples

In a hotel, for example, the rooms often differ, so separate checklists can be developed for single rooms, doubles and suites.

The top half of the list might include all the tasks that must be performed in the room each day: beds made, trash emptied, etc. The lower left quadrant might show tasks to be completed every week: carpets shampooed, etc. The lower right quadrant shows monthly tasks.

The pace and quality standards might be set by asking three people to do everything on the daily list in similar rooms quickly, but without breaking into a sweat. (This is a "no sweat standard.") The average time becomes the pace standard. The weekly and monthly items will each have their own time standards. On days that weekly and monthly items must be completed in addition to the daily tasks, the appropriate amount of time is added to the room's standard.

The housekeepers can then distribute the checklists among themselves, ensuring that everyone's load is fair, given the length of the shift and the amount of time each room will require that day.

Good results also have been achieved when engineers in manufacturing settings have used checklists to teach operators how to do preventive and other minor maintenance on their machinery. These checklists might include: a flow chart that allows the operator to diagnose minor problems; the sequence of steps to take for corrective action; and suggested standards for performance time. With these checklists, operators can avoid or diminish equipment downtime delays—the lists increase their control over the resources necessary to meet their overall performance expectations.

Creating Checklists for Routine Tasks

Take a few minutes to create a checklist for one of the key Routine tasks you want to do in a Breakthrough System. Refer to the box on page 89 if your checklist is fairly simple. Then, create a second one for a very detailed task.

Keep the Tracking Systems Informal and Self-Monitored

Important: Tracking systems should be kept informal; they shouldn't be part of the formal performance-evaluation system or collected in personnel files. Tracking systems are for self-monitored performance feedback, to help us manage our own performance. They are most effective when they are used "in the moment" of our work, and we can play with them more freely if we don't load them up with all the heavy implications of performance appraisal.

Make the system as much fun as you like, and at the end of the day, do whatever you like with the records.

Summary: The Quest for Perfection

Routine tasks, by definition, are the ones we know the most about; they are predictable. These are the tasks easiest to get under control by creating simple Breakthrough Systems. But we must not

Sample Checklist for a Routine Task

Cleaning Conference Rooms

Estimated time: 20 minutes

Time In _____ Time Out _____

- ❑ Collect all trash
- ❑ Stack dirty dishes on serving table for catering
- ❑ Clean ash trays; stack on side table
- ❑ Wipe blackboards
- ❑ Vacuum carpet
- ❑ Dust tables
- ❑ Arrange chairs around each table
- ❑ Stack extra chairs in back corner
- ❑ Return leftover articles (notebooks, pens, etc.) to reception desk

let our familiarity and ease of control lead us into ignoring the importance of Routine tasks.

Routine tasks are always at the center of every organization's life. They are the heart of the operation and the very purpose for which an organization exists. No organization can continue to survive without performing its Routine tasks with great reliability.

Furthermore, it is only Routine tasks—those we thoroughly know and control—that allow us to achieve perfection! We can't even define what perfection is for an output until we have been producing it for some time, in large quantities, for a variety of applications. Then—with information from customers, statistical and other scientific analysis, and automation—we can create processes that produce perfect outputs!

When we do Routine tasks perfectly, we deliver our outputs with such dependability and convenience that our customers tend to take us for granted. Their delight is often expressed only in their unconscious dependence. We can actually take pride in the fact that our customers don't have to bring us to mind. But we must always be mindful of our own importance as we perform these tasks.

Every day, in millions of ways, our society relies upon such perfect products and services—they become part of the unconscious assumptions upon which our society operates. Through the performance of Routine tasks, we come as close to perfection as we ever will in our lives. And so many count on us to pursue this perfection relentlessly! Our outputs are part of the foundation upon which our society's quality of life rests.

Appendix

Answers to the self-test on page 79 about performance expectation statements for Routine Tasks. (Compare with your notes.)

1. Write as many pages as I can in three hours every morning.

This statement only names an output (pages of writing); it fails to address any of the pace or quality issues.

2. Write three pages per day, as quickly as I can.

This statement names an output (page) and a quantity (three), but the time standard is vague. It is actually "every day" but this is blurred by the phrase "as quickly as I can." No quality descriptors are included.

3. Load and unload my two machines three times per shift.

This statement describes a process (loading and unloading) rather than an output. Technically this expectation could be met by simply "going through the motions." It does not make a commitment to producing outputs of any kind.

4. Satisfy all customers who come to my teller window every day.

This statement describes a desired customer response, not an output. As a result, the performance expectations are left very unclear.

There are lots of ways to "satisfy customers," many of which have little to do with the task at hand. The quantity "all who come to my window every day" might permit some wide variations in performance, too—spending half an hour chatting with each customer, for example. Others standing in line will go to someone else's window and, according to the terms of this expectation, their dissatisfaction doesn't count because they didn't "come to my window."

Only by describing the outputs we will deliver (the pace and quality of transactions) can we clarify the expectations enough to keep our relationships with customers and fellow workers in order.

5. *Do my work so that the quality inspector will be happy.*

As in item 4, this statement names a vague process (do my work) and describes a customer response (a happy quality inspector) rather than an output.

6. *Every 30 minutes, stuff 150 labeled envelopes with a letter and all the required enclosures.*

Almost. This statement includes everything but a description of accuracy—quantity (150), outputs (stuffed envelopes), timeliness (every 30 minutes) and completeness (with letter and all enclosures).

But what if the letter is personally addressed and the name and address on the letter don't match those on the envelope? And what if the letter is folded in an unprofessional way? These issues of accuracy are very important. Rather than describe them in this statement, it might be useful to have a list of style rules—like the process specifications used to set expectations for machine operators. Then we can refer to the style.

To bring this statement up to speed, rewrite it like so:

Every 30 minutes, stuff 150 labeled envelopes with a letter and all the required enclosures, *according to style #7.*

7. *Draw and verify 10 circuits per week.*

This statement has it all! Quantity (10), outputs (circuits), timeliness (per week), quality and accuracy ("verified" refers to a test the circuit-designer performs to ensure that the circuits are drawn completely and accurately) are addressed.

Breaking Through to Invention with Projects

• • • •

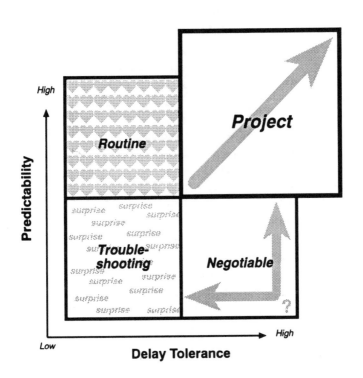

Overview

This chapter continues the discussion of how to create Breakthrough Systems for different types of tasks. Having practiced on our most familiar and repetitive tasks, we are now ready to explore ways of accomplishing Breakthrough Systems for Project tasks.

Projects are a little more difficult to manage because they set out to accomplish something original. They always aim at making a change: i.e., delivering an output that is at least partly new. Because the outputs are unique, the rest of the system also will be unique. There are special inputs, special procedures and combinations of procedures, anxious and uncertain customers and different measures for determining the pace and quality of performance.

This chapter reviews methods that Project planners have developed to gain control over some of these unique qualities. These methods help a Project planner set realistic overall objectives, schedules and budgets for any given Project. But if we are actually to manage ourselves well as we perform Project tasks, we must go much further than most Project planners do.

If we can get our Project work into Breakthrough Systems so that we can work on it a little every day, we can make an enormous difference in our organizations. Project work is what makes organizations innovative. It is how companies develop, test and introduce new or complex products and services. There is no better way to accelerate this process than for each of us to manage ourselves better when doing Project Tasks.

We've all seen plenty of Projects that weren't completed on time or within budget. Everyone may have been working hard, but things just didn't come together as expected. Project slippage is very expensive—in terms of both actual dollars spent and opportunities lost in the marketplace. Recent industrial history is littered with stories of good products that got to market too late. And associated with each of these stories is usually another story of restructuring, layoffs, takeovers, bankruptcy.

The market now expects high-quality, customized products and services in rapid response to demand. Projects are the means by which we can respond to these conditions. And to do Projects well, we must do them in Breakthrough Systems.

Key Concepts

◆ Expectations for the results of Projects should be described in three ways:
  – the *change* the Project is intended to make;
  – the *customer* who is expected to use this change; and
  – the *deadline* for the Project's completion.
◆ Project planning is not complete until the tasks are expressed in terms of *monthly deliverables* for the current year and *weekly deliverables* for the current month.
◆ We can get feedback about how we are doing on Projects by using informal tracking systems, such as:
  – Gantt charts;
  – daily to-do lists; and
  – weekly done/not done meetings.

Possible Activities

◆ Evaluate some Project goal statements.
◆ Build (or review) a rough Gantt chart for a Project that we are currently doing.
◆ Identify weekly deliverables for the current month of that Project.

Projects—One of a Kind

Whenever we intend to invent something new or to make a change, our work takes the form of a Project. The Project can be very large-scale and involve many years of effort (e.g., designing a lunar lander), or it may just require a few hours or days of work (e.g., producing a newsletter).

The most distinguishing feature of Projects is that they are always at least partially unique—the objective is to produce an original output. Though we may spend an entire career working on similar Projects, we don't generally repeat any single Project in all its detail: each one stands alone.

Often the goal of a Project is to design a product or process that will be transferred to the routine part of an organization's performance. This happens, for example, when design engineers hand off their designs to manufacturers, or when a quality-improvement team completes its problem-solving activity and implements a better new process. Although the design or problem-solving activity is a Project task, the output is a change—generally an improvement—in the organization's routine work.

Routine tasks are the heart of an organization's work, and Projects allow organizations to renew, improve or expand the products and services they routinely provide. In this sense, Projects are the creative side of work—the source of innovation and change.

Typical Projects

- ◆ Writing a book
- ◆ Designing a computer microprocessor
- ◆ Constructing an office building
- ◆ Designing a work-flow process
- ◆ Preparing a budget
- ◆ Developing a new pharmaceutical or vaccine
- ◆ Conducting a cost analysis
- ◆ Projecting cash flow
- ◆ Conducting a market study
- ◆ "Ramping up" a new product in production
- ◆ Developing a new training program
- ◆ Choosing a new software program
- ◆ Building a new team
- ◆ Restructuring an organization
- ◆ Developing a career
- ◆ Preparing a sales proposal

Cooperation Is Crucial

Because Projects are always at least partly unique, they usually involve uncertainty and learning. As we perform part of a Project task, we may confront problems that are not just new to ourselves, but new to the whole world. To solve these problems, all the methods of scientific inquiry may be required. New methodologies may have to be developed. And the Project team may need to think together for long periods of time to find appropriate interpretations, associations and applications for the information they discover.

In some cases, workers must have many years of formal education and practical experience before they can manage projects competently. We call such people professionals or knowledge workers. They show lots of initiative and can make well-informed judgments about the new information they discover and the methods they develop. Computers enable these professionals to pursue Project goals in ever-greater levels of complexity and detail. Knowledge workers are thus on the leading edge of discovery and revolutionary change. Consequently, their work is often characterized by genuine uncertainty and mystery.

Some professionals take unnecessary advantage of this uncertainty. They make all their work appear as mysterious and incomprehensible as possible! Such people seem to work from the assumption that they're only *really* good at what they do if they are operating at levels of complexity and uncertainty that "ordinary" people couldn't begin to understand. Being misunderstood is part of the costume these people believe they must wear as they play their heroic roles: "brilliant but otherworldly scientist," "lone ranger," "artiste." And they may become righteously indignant when others insist upon clarity, specificity and commitment to concrete outputs and deadlines.

The reality of "knowledge work," however, is that it requires a great deal of human interdependence. Information made available by computers is so vast and complex that no individual in any field can possibly master it all; the work must be done by combinations of minds working in concert. Intellectual teamwork is now the source of almost all great new discoveries and inventions.

And interdependence is driven even further by economic reality. The faster an idea or invention can be practically applied—i.e., made Routine—the greater its economic value. Teams can accomplish complex Projects faster than individuals. Concurrent engineering and parallel processing are the way of life in high-tech industries where new products must be developed, perfected and brought to market in shorter and shorter cycles. Professional recognition and rewards in the marketplace depend on the skillful coordination of knowledge work in these industries.

Thus, professional competence must include skill at cooperation as well as intellectual expertise. Professionals who expect or strive to be left alone are moving toward the sidelines of their fields, not toward the center of action. The speed and complexity of modern work require us to be very clear about our objectives and our current status in relation to those objectives. Professionals must, therefore, emerge from behind the veil of mystery and begin developing Breakthrough Systems for their Project work. Like everyone else, professionals must be accountable and skillful in dealing with their Role Sets.

The Pattern of Project Failure

We Don't Participate in Planning

Here's a typical scenario. Those of us who will be involved in executing a Project aren't asked to get involved until after the planning has been done. The plan may seem unrealistic to us, but rather than argue about it, we just get started on our part. We do our best, giving the task careful thought and often working extra hours.

At the first monthly status review, we report that we are working hard on the Project and, as far as we can tell, the work is being done as quickly and efficiently as possible. That is all we can reasonably report at this stage. Our part of the Project won't be completed for some time, and we won't know how all the parts will work together or whether everything will occur on schedule until more of the subtasks are completed and linked. In the early stages, we're doing everything we know to do, so we assume things are going well. Each month we report that the plan appears to be on schedule.

Nasty Surprises, Expensive Adjustments

Near the end of our part of the Project, however—usually two weeks before a milestone—we notice that the amount of work remaining will require more time than planned. We ask for an emergency status review to report the shocking findings. Other

people have already begun preparing to take the work we're supposed to hand off according to schedule, because we've been
reporting all along that we would probably meet the deadline.

Now the Project faces the added cost of down time while people
wait for us, or resources must be reallocated to help us finish the
work. Sometimes millions of dollars are at stake or the whole life of
the Project is threatened. The emergency status review is an intense
and uncomfortable meeting in which tempers flare, and by the light
of that fire a search is conducted for people to blame.

Blaming and Closer Scrutiny

Project leaders want to blame the workers for being slow or
dishonest in reporting; workers want to blame the leaders for
making such a stupid and unrealistic plan in the first place. Only
when the people who must be blamed have been identified and their
careers branded with some mark of shame, can attention return to
the Project and any necessary adjustments to the plan. The deadline
is extended, or more people, equipment or other resources are
added.

Project leaders also start requiring more frequent status reviews—weekly now, instead of monthly. Workers usually interpret
this as micro-management or a sign of distrust. But we resume our
work with every intention of satisfying the new schedule and
redeeming ourselves in the eyes of the Project team. We work even
harder and have every reason to report at the weekly status reviews
that things are going better.

More Missed Milestones

Two weeks before the new milestone, we are shocked to make
the same discovery: We're not going to make it! The problems in our
work are quite disturbing! Tests show that things weren't done
according to the designs, and even things that were done right aren't
fitting together as planned.

The new emergency status review will spend a lot of time trying
to sort it all out. Are the designers or the implementers to blame?
Why didn't the Project leaders account for these typical problems
when they originally established the schedule? After the second
round of blame and career assassination, the deadline will be

extended again, and/or more people, equipment and resources will be loaded into the Project.

These unpleasant discoveries and the ceremonies of blame are typically repeated many times during the life of a large-scale Project.

Project Slippage

In California's Silicon Valley during the early 1980s, this process typically continued until the Project had exceeded its budget and time constraints by about 250 percent. A Project expected to cost $1 million and to be completed in 12 months typically cost $2.5 million and took 30 months. In the early 1990s, slippage has decreased—Projects typically exceed their budgets and deadlines by 150 percent—and the ceremonies of blame continue.

These statistics on Project slippage aren't very impressive, although we are improving decade by decade. If our organizations are to survive in an economic environment that is increasingly competitive and fast-paced, we must learn to be accurate in estimating Project costs and deadlines.

This is why we must get Project work into a Breakthrough System.

Setting Goals and Weekly Deliverables—A Path to Creativity

Remember that the Task Grid defines Projects as tasks that are both highly predictable and tolerant of delays. That seldom seems true to workers involved in Projects that have exceeded their deadlines and budgets. The way most Projects are managed, they seem completely *un*predictable, and no one shows any tolerance for delays.

The reason the Task Grid defines them as predictable, however, is that Projects can be planned. Through planning, we can make Project performance more predictable. And Projects are delay-tolerant because when we set the deadlines, we can deliberately build *slack time* into all the appropriate steps. Slack time should be built into the schedule when a step involves uncertainty and requires learning. The Project deadline then becomes a realistic statement about when the entire effort will be finished, *including* allowances for probable delays at various steps.

Establishing the Project Plan

As with Routine tasks, the first step toward Breakthrough Performance for a Project is to set clear expectations about the results to be achieved. These expectations should include the following three elements:

1. The *change* the Project is intended to make.
2. The *customer* who is expected to use this change.
3. The *deadline* for the Project's completion.

We need to state expectations for the Project as a whole and for all subtasks within it. Clarifying these expectations depends on effective planning, which has five steps: baselining, goal setting, task analysis, scheduling and budgeting.

This chapter is not intended to be a comprehensive discussion of Project planning. Instead, it looks at how we can *use* the elements of a Project plan to help ourselves create Breakthrough Systems.

Setting the Project Goal

Describing the Change To Be Made

The first steps of Project planning involve defining the change the Project will make. Good planners begin by asking "What do customers require?" Early in the process, these planners consult with their customers and with reliable representatives of the professional team that will do the work, to assess current conditions and determine the need for change. The Project goal statement then defines the change to be made. For example:

◆ An office building will stand on what is now a vacant lot.

◆ A computer microprocessor will perform three times more calculations than any existing chip at twice the speed.

◆ We will know the size of the market for our product where once we had only a hopeful guess.

◆ We will have a career plan where once we were victims of mysterious labor-market forces.

But a statement of change is not enough—the goal statement must also identify the *customer* for the change.

Identifying the Customer

The goal statement must say how the change will be used, by whom and for what purpose. In essence, this is the Project's set of quality requirements. These requirements can be summarized briefly in the goal statement and are usually elaborated elsewhere in a complete set of specifications. This description of intended use is a way to ensure that the Project team doesn't forget the real world where customers must find their work helpful.

It may seem unnecessary to remind professionals how their Project results are to be used or applied. But millions of dollars worth of effort often are wasted when real-world applications (and obstacles) are not considered and addressed before a Project begins. Consider the following examples:

- ◆ On the 17th floor of a bank headquarters, several million dollars worth of the world's best training programs sit unused on shelves. Many of these programs won prizes from associations of training professionals. But they have never been used at this bank beyond the initial pilot-testing phase. Why? "Because managers of departments for which the programs were developed don't feel the need to use them," says the Training Director. "Furthermore, the programs are so complex that they need extremely skilled trainers to make them work."

- ◆ At a cost of millions, a leading manufacturer installed an electronic-mail system and personal computers on the desks of every employee. The potential for increased productivity in administrative and management tasks seemed incontestable. But less than 14 percent of the personal computers are actually being used more than once a week. Almost no one uses the electronic mail system because so few people actually read their mail regularly. Why is this happening? "Our people refuse to come into the computer age," says the Director of Information Systems. "We've done all the training, but computer phobia remains."

- ◆ A public shelter Project was supposed to be the answer to a major city's problem of homelessness. But three years after it was completed, tenants are deserting their quarters and returning to the streets. Why? "They find life in the shelter a bedlam rife with thievery," says the Director of Housing. "Believe it or not, they prefer the relative privacy and security of the streets."

◆ A videocassette recorder has more features than any other on the market, but almost no one is buying it. Why? "People are intimidated by all the buttons," the designer says. "All they can handle is a simple way to play the movie videos they rent."

◆ An audio system reproduces a full spectrum of sound with extraordinary precision—the highest quality ever available. It's not selling much. Why? "It's expensive," says the Sales Director. "It turns out there aren't many people willing to pay for an opportunity to point to their stereo system and tell their friends it's reproducing sounds they can't hear."

In each of these cases, the professionals who designed the products and services did "quality professional work." They can prove it by showing the professional awards they've received. The reason the products aren't being put to more use, they say, is that customers are uneducated, unreasonable and/or ungrateful. "Our work is excellent," they maintain, "it's just a little ahead of its time."

To prevent this disconnection between advanced professional work and its customers, the Project goal statement must include a description of how the expected result will be used. Naming the customers and the extent to which the Project will meet their needs forces us out of intellectual isolation and thrusts us into a relationship with our customers from the beginning. We may do something less technically perfect as a result of this relationship, but in the long run, our talents won't be entirely wasted on creativity that no one uses.

Setting the Pace and Deadlines

Planners complete the Project goal statement by determining a Project's *pace* of change. To provide this specification, they move through Task Analysis, Scheduling and Budgeting—steps three, four and five of the planning process—asking:

◆ What steps must be taken?

◆ What uncertainties and risks exist at each step?

◆ Can we get the expertise and other resources we require?

◆ Can we do it soon enough?

From these inquiries will emerge a deadline and a schedule. The deadline becomes part of the goal statement—the Project's overall pace requirement. The schedule then elaborates on that overall pace requirement by setting the pace for each subtask.

Ideally, the deadline emerges after all the best estimates of time required for each step have been added up, including allowances for uncertainties and learning time. In reality, however, the market and competition often determine when the window of opportunity will be open. Missing this window may render the Project worthless. So the window becomes the deadline, and the Project planners have no option but to plan backwards from that date. If they cannot find a way to complete the work on time, their only option may be to drop the whole idea.

One of the other results of Project planning, then, is a feasibility test. It is important to remember that the decision to undertake a Project is always discretionary; we don't *have to* do it. We do it because we feel a need and believe that we can satisfy that need. If we didn't believe it were possible to make a constructive change, we wouldn't bother planning the Project. Uncertainties and risks may be involved, but if we thought these were impossible to overcome, we wouldn't be so foolish as to attempt the task.

Example of a Complete Project Goal Statement

"Implement the new information-retrieval system for all field service representatives in Milwaukee according to the design specifications of proposal #4 by March 31, 1996."

Testing Your Understanding

Following are two sample Project Goal Statements. After each statement, the pace (deadline) and quality requirements (change and usefulness) are listed. After you've had a chance to look them over, test your own understanding on the two additional goal statements that follow. See whether each goal statement adequately identifies the Project's pace, change and usefulness. (Answers are in the Appendix at the end of this chapter beginning on page 117.)

Samples

Goal 1: "Design to production readiness the Z45 computer chip, according to architectural specifications, by the third quarter of 1996."

Pace (deadline): Third quarter of 1996.

Quality

> **Change:** "Design the Z45 computer chip."
>
> **Customers:**
>
> ◆ "According to architectural specifications" (which describe what the chip must do for its external customers); and
>
> ◆ "To production readiness." (This means that more than a first silicon sample must be created; the expected result is a de-bugged chip ready to be produced on a manufacturing line. This requirement ties the design engineers to their internal customers in the company's manufacturing division.)

Goal 2: "Reduce the production cycle time (from the time the order is received to the time it is shipped) from 21 days to 2 days, with a return rate of less than 1 percent, by the first quarter of 1995."

Pace (deadline): First quarter of 1995.

Quality

> **Change:** "Reduce production cycle time from 21 days to 2 days."
>
> **Customers:**
>
> ◆ "From the time the order is received to the time it is shipped." (This connects the manufacturing people to their internal customers: those who take orders and those who package and ship the product to external customers.)
>
> ◆ "With a return rate of less than 1 percent." (The process must not only be fast, but useful to the customer 99 percent of the time.)

Your Turn

Goal A: "Prepare the annual budget recommendations in a zero-based format, for executive staff's budget-approval sessions, by week 45."

Pace (deadline):

Quality

Change:

Customers:

Goal B: "Design, develop, pilot and transfer to Corporate Training the *Problem-Solving Selling Skills* course by the end of fiscal year 1995, so that it can be delivered to 80 percent of the loan officers in 20 branches."

Pace:

Quality

Change:

Customers:

For Breakthrough Performance, Establish Weekly Deliverables

A good Project goal statement is the very important and necessary first step in Project planning, but by itself, it won't prevent all the problems discussed above. The pace and quality requirements must be further broken down into detailed sets of sub-tasks, which the individual contributors to the Project will perform according to sub-deadlines. This is the purpose of steps three and four of the Project-planning process—Task Analysis and Scheduling. Good planners always involve individual contributors in these steps.

First, all necessary sub-tasks must be analyzed and a schedule developed that determines when each task must be completed to meet the overall Project deadline. Most plans for large Projects only go as far as scheduling sub-tasks in monthly increments. Before Breakthrough Performance is possible, the planning must go further—to *weekly deliverables*.

Each event in the Project plan must be broken into concrete deliverables. The definition of *concrete* is a tangible item that passes the "Look, Ma!" test (see Chapter 3 for details). A Project *deliverable* is an output to which we can point and say "done" or "not done." A deliverable that is "done" meets the quality requirements of the internal or external customer. Two or more people can see and agree that the output is or is not done. It's not relevant to say that a deliverable is "40 percent done." This kind of talk is usually so subject to interpretation and argument that it is not useful.

Sample Weekly Deliverables

- ◆ A circuit schematic designed and verified
- ◆ Ten pages of the first draft of Chapter 3
- ◆ Budget for the Auto Department of the Fleet Division
- ◆ A list summarizing retail prices for various database software packages
- ◆ Projected flow of weekly sales revenue from standard products
- ◆ Installation of a new gas line in Section 2 of the plant
- ◆ Design for Module Two of the class on Effective Meetings
- ◆ Design for collecting market data re: rear pockets with Velcro closures
- ◆ Resumés of the top 20 job applicants selected
- ◆ Complete answer sheet for the Occupational Preferences Test
- ◆ A list of three problems that Company X can solve with our services, backed with data from interviews

Establishing a Delivery Schedule

Beware of any Project plan that expresses expectations in terms of "person hours" to be spent on particular tasks or events. Typical computer programs for Project Management usually create reports that compare "person-hours expended" with "hours budgeted." But this is a cost control measure useful only for accounting. It doesn't contribute to getting us into Breakthrough Systems. The amount of time spent on a Project may bear little relation to the results accomplished. To know about results, we have to talk about them as concrete deliverables. Each person working on a Project team must be able to deliver a completed piece of the work to which everyone can point and say "done" or "not done."

It is very important to keep dissecting the events of a Project plan until they can be expressed as outputs an individual contributor can get "done" in one week. If several deliverables can be done together in one week by a single contributor, that's even better.

No deliverable should require more than two weeks to get "done." If one will definitely need more time than that, the deliverable should be broken down further into sub-deliverables. Project work must be set on a "horizon" that we can see clearly and confidently, which is two weeks at most. After that, the probability of unforeseen changes and slippage increases significantly. We're most reliable in estimating accomplishments in weekly intervals, so that is the ideal horizon.

If you have a large task, one that will take 6 months to complete, for example, don't bother breaking it directly into 24 weekly sub-tasks, however. That would be a futile exercise, because conditions will change significantly during any three-month period. Inevitably, replanning will be necessary, and too much detail in future stages of the plan will make that process unnecessarily difficult.

Instead, break the six-month task into *monthly* deliverables, then break the first month's deliverable (or cluster of deliverables) into weekly deliverables.

Begin work on the first week's deliverables. At the end of that week, hold a team status review to see what is actually "done" and "not done." Then modify expectations for the next three weeks as necessary. At the end of the month, hold a team meeting to replan the entire upcoming month in terms of weekly deliverables for each member of the Project team.

Although a Project team using this system will be able to say whether its weekly deliverables are "done" or "not done," this ability does not mean that the team has removed all uncertainty from its performance of tasks. Unexpected delays or discoveries still occur. Also, saying that an item is "not done" gives no information about when the task *will* be "done."

A weekly "done/not done" checkup does remove ambiguity from the team's discussion of what actually has been completed and what is available for others to use or work upon. A weekly summary of "done" tasks also gives the team a sense of concrete achievement and makes the status reviews a source of reliable information, not just a place where people guess everything is going all right. This sense of accomplishment and confidence can, in turn, trigger enormous breakthroughs in the team's overall Project performance.

Of course, weekly reports about deliverables "done" and "not done" can't tell the whole story of what is happening in a complex Project. But such reports do make intelligent cooperation among team members possible. The reports also help the team identify problems early, so resources can be focused on these areas right away. Overloads on certain members of the team can be spotted and work can be reallocated to avoid bottlenecks. In general, corrective action begins earlier everywhere in the Project, and this prevents the disastrous surprises that can shatter careers and destroy team members' trust and confidence in one another.

Clear expectations, stated in terms of concrete, weekly deliverables, are only the first step toward Breakthrough Performance for a Project task. These expectations set us up to create the second part: self-monitored performance feedback systems.

Tracking Weekly Performance—Secret to Cycle Time Reduction

Almost all complex Projects are tracked with some sort of computer software. Usually, however, these tracking systems apply only to major tasks. They are seldom used to analyze all the minor sub-tasks in ways that would provide immediate, reliable performance feedback for individual contributors. Many tracking systems could be useful in this way, but Project managers haven't yet seen fit to adjust the applications to suit this purpose.

Typically, computerized Project schedules operate in monthly increments and are updated monthly. This does not provide useful performance feedback to people working on the Project day to day. It is not immediate enough. Monthly updates do have some value; they may help team members stay aware of the Project's overall status, for example. They may also allow team members to assess the consequences of this month's performance on overall Project goals. The software can quickly recalculate the scheduling and budgetary consequences. It also can identify the Project's "critical path"—the sequence of interdependent events that cannot tolerate delay without extending the Project's overall deadline. This is important information for upper-level project management, but it does not provide *performance feedback* for individual contributors on the project team.

To get into a Breakthrough System, we must know how we are doing *every day* of the current week. We must be able to go home every night with a pretty good idea of whether we'll be able to hand off this week's deliverables by Friday afternoon. Most current computer tracking systems don't help much at this level. So we can fall back on an old, but very adequate, tracking system called *Gantt charts*.

Gantt Charts: Tried and True

Henry L. Gantt invented this system for representing Project work early in the 20th century. The beauty of Gantt charts is that they are simple, but capable of displaying a large amount of Project data. Almost anyone can learn to read a Gantt chart in about 15 minutes (including those who are not fully literate, or whose native language differs from the one the Project team uses most commonly). Most people can also learn to develop Gantt charts for Project planning in about 45 minutes. Refer to the sample on page 111.

Along the Gantt chart's vertical axis, key events in the Project timeline are listed in rough chronological order, from top to bottom. In our case, we want the list in terms of deliverables.

The horizontal axis is a timeline. In our case, the timeline should show a month in terms of days or weeks.

For each deliverable on the vertical axis, we draw a horizontal *duration line* to show when work on that deliverable is planned to begin and how long we expect the work to continue until it is done. This graphic system shows which deliverables can be worked on concurrently and which will have to wait until others are done. Interdependencies between deliverables can be represented by connecting appropriate duration lines with dotted lines.

A list of the individual contributors working on the Project can be added at the bottom of the chart and assigned different codes (letters, numbers or colors). By adding these codes to the duration lines, a reader can see who is working on each deliverable. (You can

Sample Gantt Chart

Key Steps	January 1st 2nd 3rd 4th	February 1st 2nd 3rd 4th	March 1st 2nd 3rd 4th

Key Steps

	January				February				March			
	1st	2nd	3rd	4th	1st	2nd	3rd	4th	1st	2nd	3rd	4th
Preliminary Plan	a	▲										
Input from Users		a	b	d	▲	c	e					
Approval from Users						a	▲					
Design Computer Program							a	▲				
De-bug Program									a	▲		
Implement Program									★			

Resources

   a   Earl

   b   5-8 Dissatisfied Users

   c   5-8 Dissatisfied Users

   d   10-15 Satisfied Users

   e   10-15 Satisfied Users

   ▲   Diana for progress checks

A Gantt chart with weekly deliverables listed along the vertical axis and a timeline along the horizontal axis.

also assign machines in the same way, and then you'll know who is doing a task and what machinery they're using.)

At status review meetings, the team draws a vertical check line down the chart to show which week has just passed. Then the team can look at each duration line that was supposed to stop before the current week's check line and determine whether it is "done" or "not done." It's always a good idea to celebrate items that are done on time. Corrective action can be taken on deliverables "not done"— the team should define the problem and reallocate resources, if necessary, to keep the Project on schedule.

Create a Gantt chart for a key Project in your own workplace.

Weekly Team Meetings

Weekly team meetings are not intended to be a peer-pressure tactic, although at first some of us may feel uncomfortable and self-conscious about them. The real purpose of making "done/not done" reports in front of the whole team is to get everyone out of isolation.

Very often, when we're facing a particular problem, we'll find that someone else on the team has already encountered and solved it. If that someone doesn't know we're having the problem, however, we may be left to work on it alone for days.

Many professionals tend to think that their problems are unique. "If they were common problems," the reasoning goes, "I would already know how to solve them." Such people sometimes act as if it is their individual destiny to solve these "unique" problems alone.

If we admit the problems to our peers once a week, however, they will often be able to tell us immediately where we can find answers and assistance. This helps us avoid wasting our talents on reinventing known solutions. That's the real intent of these weekly meetings.

For a team of eight or nine professionals, the weekly meeting *shouldn't take more than 15 minutes*. It's not a time for in-depth technical problem-solving; if that becomes necessary, the issue probably should be handled by a task force or by individual tutorials after the meeting. The purposes of the weekly "done/not done" meeting are simply to: acknowledge good work; identify problems and corrective actions to be taken; accumulate reliable information about the Project's status this week; and make any necessary adjustments in deliverables planned for the next week. "Ceremonies of blame" never help.

To-Do Lists—The Daily Discipline

Even a weekly meeting is not a frequent enough feedback loop to cause a Breakthrough in Project performance. Our ability to adapt and learn—to make Breakthroughs—depends upon very short feedback loops. The only way to create a fast, flexible, highly productive system is to ensure that the people in it have immediate information about how their performance meshes with the organization's overall goals. When this occurs, we usually find that personal productivity leaps to a higher level, and as this happens for more team members, the whole group makes a Breakthrough. Thus, individual team members must have frequent enough feedback to manage themselves and one another *every day*. This isn't difficult to do when we know what we're supposed to deliver by Friday.

Most people use a simple daily "to-do" list. As we come to our work stations on Monday morning, for example, we look at our weekly deliverables and make a list of what we will need to do each day to get everything done by Friday. Then we start with Monday's list, and check off the items as we go. Tuesday, we add anything left over from Monday to the current day's list. If it looks like we're already getting into trouble, we go to our colleagues or supervisor for help.

When Friday comes, we may not have all our deliverables "done"; but we rarely have any nasty surprises. We've already been taking corrective action, and our efforts are respectable. Early warning allows for early corrective action, usually at minimal expense. Stress is minimized, and our whole brains keep working.

This is not just a fantasy or an ideal. It really happens. Consider the following real-life examples.

Some Success Stories

A Project to design a new computer microprocessor involved more than 100 engineers at a major semiconductor manufacturing company. The Project plan called for a 12-month effort; the chip had to be ready for the customer to display at one of the industry's most important trade shows.

Three months into the effort, the computer tracking system indicated that the Project was already six weeks behind schedule. If the team missed the trade show deadline, the product would be worthless in the market. If the tracking system was correct, a way had to be found immediately to either catch up or to cancel the Project.

The Project leader decided to use the next two weeks to see whether he could create a Breakthrough. The Project's executive team was enlisted in the effort and reviewed the current situation. They then held a special meeting with all first-line managers, explained the situation and described what would be required to meet the deadline:

- ♦ Every contributing engineer would have to work on weekly deliverables.
- ♦ Supervisors would conduct informal checkups with every engineer twice a week.
- ♦ Each engineering team would hold a weekly meeting for "done/not done" reports.
- ♦ A revised computer system would track the Project in terms of deliverables.

The first-line managers all committed themselves to these practices. The Project leader then held "all hands" meetings with the engineers. He explained that the Project appeared to be in jeopardy and that a more reliable system of performance feedback might allow the Project to get back on track. He reviewed the new feedback systems.

The engineers immediately met with their first-line managers and set weekly deliverables for the next four weeks. They created a simple reporting system in matrix format. A deliverable was listed on each horizontal row of the matrix. Each vertical column represented a week of the Project. An "X" in the appropriate row and column indicated when each deliverable was due. The last column listed the name of the engineer working on each deliverable. (See illustration below.)

Matrix of Weekly Deliverables

Deliverable	Week 1	Week 2	Week 3	Week 4	Person
P1	X				Avtar
P2	X				Avtar
Z1	X				Jane
Z2		X			Jane
Z3			X		Jorge
Z4				X	Jorge
Y1		X			Kim
Y2				X	Kim

Team Leader's Checklist for Creating a Breakthrough System for Projects

1. Working with the team members as a group:
   a. Break the next month's work into weekly deliverables.
   b. Assign weekly deliverables to individuals.
2. Check informally with each individual twice per week.
3. At the end of each week, hold "done/not done" meetings.
4. At the same meeting, review the next week's deliverables; make necessary adjustments.
5. Begin the next week.
6. At the end of the month, return to step 1.

Three days later, the first weekly "done/not done" meetings were held. Engineers needed assurances that these reports would not be part of their formal performance reviews—"done/not done" is a woefully inadequate measure of engineering skill. But the engineers were quickly taking up the new Project-management practices.

By the end of the second week, it was obvious that productivity was rising dramatically. The executive team decided to continue with the Project. Six weeks later the Project was back on track and remained there, despite serious technological surprises and hurdles that no one had been able to foresee. An evaluation at the end of the Project indicated that the engineers and managers had come to prefer the Breakthrough practices and were sure that the practices contributed mightily to the Project's success.

In another case, the team that designed the Pentium™ Processor at Intel, the Silicon Valley microchip manufacturer, also used Breakthrough practices from day one. Their extraordinarily complex and powerful chip moved into production faster than any previous generation of a similar chip. Managers and team members say that the Breakthrough practices were integral to the success of their efforts.

Matrix of Weekly Deliverables

Deliverable	Week 1	Week 2	Week 3	Week 4	Person
1					
2					
3					
4					
5					
6					
7					
8					

Your Turn: Creating a Breakthrough System for a Key Project

Create a Breakthrough System for one of your key Projects—perhaps the one that you put into a Gantt Chart earlier in this chapter. In the spaces above, assign weekly deliverables to individuals for the next four weeks. Follow the steps for creating a Breakthrough System.

Summary: Speed Equals Value

Project work is exciting and important because it creates change. It can change the landscape, improve routine processes, enhance the quality of life with new products and services and alter the political aspirations of whole nations.

The economic and social value of Projects is growing in direct relationship to the speed and precision with which they are performed. More and more, we will have to begin our Projects without knowing everything we'll need to know to complete them. We will have to learn as we go and replan on the basis of our learning. Speed in Project performance is directly related to the team's ability to learn, and learning depends upon immediate and reliable feedback. Our future in Project work lies in Breakthrough practices.

Appendix

Answers to Goal Statement Problems

Goal A: "Prepare the annual budget recommendations in zero-based format for the executive staff's budget-approval sessions by week 45."

Pace (deadline): "Week 45."

Quality

> **Change:** "Prepare the annual budget recommendations."
>
> **Customers:** "For executive staff's budget approval sessions"
>
> (The recommendations must facilitate these important decision-making meetings.); and
>
> "In zero-based format."
>
> (This format requires options for all budget items. It gives the executive staff better information about the consequences of various allocations and greater flexibility in making decisions.)

Goal B: Design, develop, pilot and transfer to Corporate Training the *Problem-Solving Selling Skills* course by the end of fiscal year 1995, so that it can be delivered to 80 percent of the loan officers in 20 branches.

Pace: "End of fiscal year 1995."

Quality

> **Change:** "Design, develop, pilot and transfer . . . *Problem-Solving Selling Skills* course."
>
> **Customers:** "So that it can be delivered to 80 percent of the loan officers in 20 branches"
>
> (This specific target audience must find the program potentially useful enough to attend the course.); and
>
> "Transfer to Corporate Training."
>
> (The current staff in Corporate Training must be able to administer and deliver the program.)

Breaking Through with Unpredictable Tasks

◆ ◆ ◆ ◆

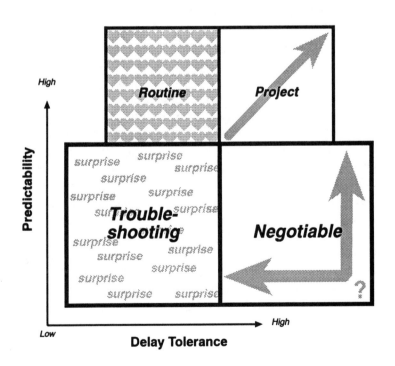

Overview

Chapters 4 and 5 covered the two predictable tasks types, Routine and Projects. This chapter explores how we can create Breakthrough Systems for the two unpredictable tasks types: Troubleshooting and Negotiable.

Troubleshooting tasks are the most unpredictable and, as explained in Chapter 3, have very little delay tolerance. Such tasks are usually emergencies of some sort—as dramatic as equipment failures and life-threatening medical emergencies, or as commonplace as telephone complaints to customer-service departments. Each incident is unique, even though some part of it may be handled with Routine procedures.

Negotiables are a mix of Troubleshooting and Project tasks, as explained in Chapter 3. They arise unexpectedly, but can be delayed if more pressing priorities must be met first. Negotiables are nonemergency unpredictables with more delay tolerance.

No matter what kind of work an organization does—even if it is very Routine production work—someone will have to be able to perform Troubleshooting and Negotiable tasks. Ordinary systems always break down, and somebody has to fix the situation in a hurry. Without good troubleshooting, no system survives for long.

When we start trying to develop Breakthrough Systems for unpredictable tasks, we are immediately confronted with what appears to be a contradiction: how can you set expectations for the unpredictable? The inputs, processes, outputs and customers are unknown until we are required to perform the tasks. We won't be able to describe specific outputs as we did when setting expectations for performance of the predictable tasks. Instead, we will have to describe, in a more general way, the kind of expertise we expect from ourselves when we are troubleshooting. We cannot predict the exact output that will be appropriate for each Troubleshooting task, but we can establish some simple measures that will tell us whether or not we know how to handle such situations. Once these measures are established, we can build the rest of the Breakthrough System.

Turning our attention to simple ways of getting immediate and reliable feedback about our performance of these unpredictable tasks, we discover that the collection of such information is not only important as performance feedback, but also as a database from which we help the organization take corrective action. Troubleshooters are especially able to make this contribution because they are always in the middle of the organization's urgent problems. They are always trying to fix the Routine and Project systems that have broken down. Keeping records of these situations allows the organization to identify the root causes of the breakdowns and design permanent solutions.

Breakthrough Systems give us a special kind of control for performing unpredictable tasks; they give us control over our own confusion and fears. Breakthrough Systems allow us to identify, locate and acquire the skills or resources we need to handle emergencies. Breakthrough Systems help us to become more competent so that we can face unpredictability and problems with greater self-assurance. Without Breakthrough Systems, these unpredictable tasks often lead to nothing but headaches and distress. With Breakthrough Systems, however, these tasks may become some of the most exciting and satisfying ones we perform.

Key Concepts

- ◆ Expectations for the performance of Troubleshooting tasks must specify four things:
  1. The response time
  2. The average solution time
  3. The percentage of problems that should stay solved after the first Troubleshooting effort
  4. Acceptable manners for the Troubleshooter
- ◆ Expectations for frequently demanded Negotiable tasks should specify the same four elements listed above, since such tasks closely resemble Troubleshooting. For less-frequently demanded Negotiable tasks, the method for describing expected results is the same as for Projects.
- ◆ Performance feedback for unpredictable tasks can be collected with informal tracking systems, such as:
  − 30-Second Reports
  − Checklists
  − Gantt Charts
  − To-Do lists

Possible Activities

- ◆ Hold a *war stories* party to identify Troubleshooting tasks in our part of the organization.
- ◆ Search for data about the frequency of Troubleshooting tasks in our part of the organization.
- ◆ Select one or more areas of Troubleshooting in which we can collect data in 30-Second Reports.
- ◆ Use existing data or 30 days of 30-Second Report data to set a standard for Troubleshooting expertise in our area of the organization.
- ◆ Establish a monthly forum in which Troubleshooters can review one another's performances of this type of task.

The Terror and Wonder of Unpredictable Tasks

This chapter discusses methods of creating Breakthrough Systems for the two types of tasks that are, by definition, unpredictable. When tackling a Troubleshooting or Negotiable task, we can never be sure what we will do until the situation actually presents itself.

Troubleshooting tasks differ from Negotiables in the amount of delay tolerance they can bear. Troubleshooting tasks are always emergencies—they jump to the top of our priority lists and must be handled immediately. Negotiable tasks permit more time for planning, organizing and delivering the required performance. We're often able to work Negotiable tasks into our priority list further from the top.

In fact, Negotiables are usually short-term projects. This is especially true if they occur infrequently—only once or twice a month. Most of what we need to create Breakthrough Systems for infrequent Negotiable tasks has been covered already in Chapter 5: Projects. We perform such tasks according to the objectives we set *when we accept them*, and we can monitor ourselves with simple Gantt charts and To-Do lists. When we finish this sort of task, we can evaluate our performance by identifying how well we delivered the necessary results and met the promised deadlines.

If Negotiables happen as often as once a week, however, we won't have time to set Project goals and maintain Gantt charts. Instead, we will have to use methods more suited to Troubleshooting, which differ significantly from the ones we use for Routine tasks or Projects.

Troubleshooting Examples

- ◆ Extinguishing fires
- ◆ Ambulance services
- ◆ 911 emergency dispatching
- ◆ Lifeguarding at the beach
- ◆ Aerial combat
- ◆ Restoring electrical power after a blackout
- ◆ Answering phones as a receptionist
- ◆ Maintaining emergency equipment
- ◆ Handling customer service tasks
- ◆ De-bugging software
- ◆ Resolving complaints in a retail shoe store
- ◆ Routing deliveries
- ◆ Cooking on a short-order grill
- ◆ Responding to hazardous-materials spillage
- ◆ Directing live TV coverage of a basketball game
- ◆ Publishing front-page news

Negotiable Examples

- ◆ Analyzing special costs
- ◆ Studying special markets
- ◆ Responding to a request for "employee of the year" nominations
- ◆ Performing surprise inspections
- ◆ Completing orders in a job-shop
- ◆ Performing automobile maintenance in a dealer's service department

- Preparing a paper on a new method for verifying logic-circuit designs
- Searching professional literature on a current topic
- Responding to a political constituent's complaint

Surprise and Distress

All unpredictable tasks do have three elements in common.

First, our response to unpredictable tasks is *reactive*—we are almost always moved into action by someone else's initiative. People come to us because they have a problem, often an emergency. Their requests usually interrupt whatever else we were doing. Our plans may be destroyed, and we may feel jerked out of control.

Second, the outputs of Unpredictable tasks depend on the particular variables of each case. Expectations cannot be stated the same way they are for Routine and Project tasks.

Third, because people requesting help are usually in trouble, they are likely to be emotionally upset. And when upset people find the Troubleshooter(s) who can or should help, their negative emotions often burst out all over. Sometimes people vent anger and blame; other times, they react with fear and the disorderly flight of panic. Unless we have a swinging brick where we ought to have a heart, we can find these emotions quite contagious.

Both the surprise of the interruption and the intensity of emotion draw us into the storm. We find ourselves believing that we've been unjustly accused and start defending ourselves. Or, we join in the panic.

Suddenly, the situation really goes out of control. What may have started as a technical problem, for example, blows into an even more complex and messy human relations situation. Before we can work on the original problem, we have to try to get over wanting to wring someone's neck!

The Thrill of the Chase

Most of us know firsthand how stressful Troubleshooting can be. For some of us, distress is our dominant memory, and we try to avoid situations where Troubleshooting is involved. Yet others love the excitement of Troubleshooting.

Within us lives the spirit of the Lone Ranger, just waiting for a cry of distress. The jolt of surprise makes our blood run thin and hot with excitement. With strains of the William Tell Overture playing in the back of our minds, we mount up confidently upon our skills and ride to the crisis seeking targets for our brilliant, silver-bullet solutions. For such people, Troubleshooting is as exciting as a video game: Problems must be solved with instant perceptions and precisely controlled reflexes. Trouble is just where the action is.

These tasks are opportunities to express our mission of helpfulness to others, sometimes at great risk and self-sacrifice. These tasks call us to rise above others' distress and abusive behavior, to create at least a temporary peace and to clear a little space where a permanent correction can be established. Thus, Troubleshooting can affect and draw upon our deepest feelings of self-esteem.

Troubleshooting also can be an act of discovery and creation. Troubleshooters stand at the frayed edges of our social processes and knowledge, dealing with our systems' failures and the unknown. With some pretty sophisticated forms of bailing wire and chewing gum, Troubleshooters help what is crumbling hold together a little longer, patch up leaks and identify the contradictions and dilemmas that become goads for intelligent progress. Troubleshooting is a kind of trailblazing; it involves discovering or making landmarks in the dim confusion, so that eventually the rest of us can pass through easily.

Defining Expertise for Troubleshooters

The Skills of Troubleshooting

Motivated Troubleshooters have the sort of personality that is attracted to the excitement of problem solving. But good Troubleshooters also have special skills:

- ◆ The ability to analyze and diagnose problems quickly
- ◆ Creativity in finding immediate solutions
- ◆ Expertise in their field
- ◆ Good physical and emotional health
- ◆ Data collection skills
- ◆ An understanding that their output is not just an emergency repair, but also information for long-term solutions

Troubleshooting is a professional activity. It requires informed judgment, initiative and the ability to tailor responses to the many unique problems that present themselves.

Troubleshooters develop and maintain their skills through continuous practice. Since they never know exactly what will be required, they must be prepared for a wide range of possibilities. Troubleshooters continuously confront themselves and one another with case studies, live simulations and practice drills to keep their responses quick and flawless.

And because dealing with unpredictable tasks involves emotional hazards, the best Troubleshooters don't just focus on maintaining their specific technical skills. They almost always work at maintaining good physical and mental shape as well. The stress of Troubleshooting can quickly take its toll on emotional and physical health. To prevent this, successful Troubleshooters practice a regimen of physical exercise and often spend lots of time with individuals and groups specifically devoted to emotional counseling and support.

The final mark of an expert Troubleshooter is skill at collecting data that can lead to long-term solutions. Most Troubleshooting work doesn't actually provide permanent solutions to problems; it usually just provides some temporary glue that holds a situation together until a more permanent solution can be found. By keeping good notes, however, Troubleshooters can eventually help identify the underlying causes of a problem. With that information, permanent corrective action can be undertaken—perhaps through a Project to redesign a Routine system.

All human communities tend to reward Troubleshooters with special compensation, attention and status. These rewards are usually well deserved. But rewards may also tempt Troubleshooters to more or less consciously perpetuate the existence of problems. Without problems, Troubleshooters have no work, no satisfaction, no glory. Some Troubleshooters resist others' efforts to get rid of problems permanently.

And some people are so accustomed to living in a state of constant crisis and panic that they simply don't know any other way to live, so they arrange their lives to continually replicate emergency conditions.

Thus, it's important to remember that an expert Troubleshooter's job is not just to make a quick fix, but to provide information that starts the process of permanent improvement. Without this final skill, Troubleshooters get trapped on a treadmill of problem solving that wears them out without creating any substantial progress. Thrills and glory may carry them through the early part of their careers, but the treadmill eventually leads to "Burnout"—fatigue accompanied by feelings of hopelessness and despair.

On the other hand, Troubleshooting can also lead to a career in management. Managers spend a lot of time Troubleshooting—they design the systems by which an organization's Routine and Project work is supposed to get done. They also stand by to deal with circumstances that interfere with those planned activities. Managers "hold things together" in emergencies, while information is gathered to help redesign systems and make permanent improvements to them.

Setting Expectations—Are You Kidding?

As always, the first step toward creating any Breakthrough System is clear expectations. But how can anyone set performance expectations for tasks that are inherently unpredictable? We won't know what the problem is until it happens. We won't know what the outputs are supposed to be until we understand the problem, and the outputs probably will vary every time. It is, in fact, impossible to prescribe the solutions a Troubleshooter invents. You can't really say much more about outputs than: "Do whatever you have to do."

A Breakthrough System does require some kind of clear expectation to guide the performer's work. For unpredictable tasks, we turn away from the outputs and focus instead on the process. We can establish rough measures for the pace and quality of a good Troubleshooting process. These measures are standards of expertise rather than descriptions of specific, desired outputs.

For Troubleshooting and frequent Negotiables, four issues must be addressed:

1. Response Time
2. Solution Time
3. First-Pass Success
4. Manner

The first two issues concern *pace*—how quickly each problem will be acknowledged and then solved. The latter two concern *quality*—how well the problem is solved on the Troubleshooter's first visit and how the Troubleshooter behaves toward customers. When we combine statements about these four issues, we can make clear for ourselves and others our understanding of the role of Troubleshooters.

For example: Be on the site of an emergency equipment failure within 15 minutes after the request for maintenance is received. Complete 80 percent of the necessary repairs within 90 minutes. Do it well enough that the same problem doesn't recur within six months. Stay calm, and report your work to the equipment's operators and their supervisor/s.

Following, each of these four elements is explained in greater detail, with more examples.

Expectations for Negotiables

If a Negotiable task occurs *frequently*, use the four Troubleshooting guidelines of:

1. Response Time
2. Solution Time
3. First-Pass Success
4. Manner

Example: Acknowledge special requests for preliminary cost studies on the same day that they are received. Complete the cost studies within 10 working days so that rework is unnecessary in 95 percent of the cases.

If a Negotiable task occurs *infrequently*, commit to performing it according to the Project goals established when you accept the task.

Example: In all cases, complete special-request cost studies according to the formats, deadlines and expenses agreed upon with the requester when the task is initiated.

Review Chapter 5 for guidelines on defining Project goals— the change to be made, the deadline and the output's usefulness to customers.

Defining Pace and Quality

Response time specifies how quickly a request for help should be acknowledged. For example:

◆ Pick up the phone before the third ring.

◆ Be at the site of an equipment failure within five minutes after the call for help.

◆ Have a vehicle moving toward the emergency within one minute of the call 95 percent of the time.

◆ Make eye contact at the service counter in the first three seconds.

◆ Don't let anyone stand in line longer than three minutes.

◆ Greet every customer as he/she enters the store.

◆ Mail a written acknowledgment of each complaint the same day it is received.

Solution time is the average time in which most problems should be solved. For example:

◆ Satisfy 85 percent of requests for information within five minutes.

◆ Restore equipment to operation within one hour 80 percent of the time.

◆ Stabilize the condition of the injured and be in transit to appropriate emergency facilities within 10 minutes of arrival, 80 percent of the time.

◆ Resolve 85 percent of complaints at the counter within two minutes.

◆ Fulfill orders within 90 seconds 90 percent of the time.

First-pass success describes the percentage of cases that should be resolved the first time that they are addressed and the amount of time solutions should last (i.e., the repair's completeness and accuracy). For example:

◆ The information given should be sufficient to keep the customer from having to call again during the same billing period.

◆ The maintenance work should survive the specified warranty period.

◆ A call for assistance from a senior mechanic should not be required in more than 10 percent of cases.

◆ All fires must be completely suppressed—no call-backs!

◆ The patient should reach the emergency room alive 95 percent of the time.

Manner refers to communications with and behavior toward customers—literally, the Troubleshooter's manners. This element is particularly important to define when the work involves personal contact with customers.

◆ At the counter, greet each customer with eye contact and a smile. As soon as possible and appropriate, use the customer's surname.

◆ Remain pleasant and polite, or excuse yourself from a situation temporarily until it is possible to regain composure.

◆ An officer should appear alert, reasonable, confident and authoritative—able and ready to use force if necessary.

◆ A clerk should be seen as one who provides information about choices and consequences, not as an adviser, director or enforcer.

Some Complete Examples

The following statements are good, complete examples of performance expectations for Troubleshooters.

◆ I will pick up the phone before the third ring and answer 80 percent of the billing inquiries within three minutes, well enough that the customer will not have to call again within the same billing period. No customer should ever have any complaint about the respectfulness with which I handle any request.

◆ I will respond by phone or fax to customer inquiries within 15 minutes of the customer's call and handle the inquiries in a way that will promote further consideration of our proposal in 80 percent of cases.

◆ I will arrive on the site of the equipment failure within five minutes of receiving the call and have the equipment back in operation within an hour in 80 percent of the cases. If the repair will take longer, I will know and inform the customer within 15 minutes of my arrival and have a Senior Maintenance Specialist on the way to the site. I will conduct myself in such a way that no one will complain about the respectfulness I showed while I worked with them.

◆ Ninety percent of the time, I will lead cross-functional, multishift de-bug teams to provide fully integrated, verified solutions within 24 hours after I receive the assignment.

Mind Your Manners!

A manufacturer of high-tech quality monitoring equipment had customers who used their equipment to measure the thickness and other characteristics of rolled steel, building insulation and paper. If the monitoring equipment failed, the whole production line would be forced to shut down. Such occurrences were always very expensive for customers, so it was important to keep the monitoring equipment in perfect working order.

To ensure this, a technical representative ("tech rep") was assigned to each machine sold. This tech rep was available via pager 24-hours per day, 50 weeks per year, to fix the machines when they broke down. When a tech rep was paged, he or she had to be on site within 15 minutes—no excuses were acceptable.

Plants ran 24 hours a day, and inevitably, emergency breakdowns happened during the night. The tech reps would arrive grumpy and "let it all hang out" while they went about doing an excellent job of fixing the equipment. Many of these tech reps had come directly from the Navy where they had developed a habit of embellishing blame with derogatory references to customers' general competence and heredity. Though they restored the equipment, they left behind work crews (and sometimes managers) who felt deeply offended and unforgiving.

After a few emergencies, customers would call and say: "Come get your equipment out of here!" The manufacturer asked what was wrong—anything with the equipment? "No," the customers would say, "We just don't like you!"

My client had to set a standard for the manner in which tech reps did their work. They were asked to commit themselves to "looking and acting pleased to be of service" and never generating complaints about their behavior on the job. Many had to go through special training—a "finishing school"—to learn how to act this way when they were actually feeling frightened, angry or insulted. But, attention to their manners paid off.

Using 30-Second Reports and Other Feedback Systems

Keeping the Big Picture in Focus

To be excellent, Troubleshooters must commit to collecting and advertising data that contribute to long-term solutions and continuous improvement in organizations.

Advertising the data is important, because the people around us may not know that we have or are building such a database and may never think to ask for it. They may suggest changes that are unworkable or uninformed, because they don't know that relevant data exist. Or they may spend a lot of time doing research that we have already completed.

Such data also can help organizations avoid a tendency to rely on *quick fixes* and instead find efficient, cost-effective long-term solutions that may involve redesigning underlying processes. Both internal and external customers will be better served by solutions more permanent than an emergency patch job. So Troubleshooters may need to add some statements like these to their performance expectations:

- ◆ I will provide to my team leader monthly summaries of my Troubleshooting activities.

- ◆ I will deliver to my supervisor a record of the time, place, source and type of interruption that I experience while I am trying to produce user manuals.

- ◆ I will E-mail to Design Engineering records of the complaints customers make about our product while I perform routine maintenance.

- ◆ I will deliver to marketing or product design a monthly record of the objections customers raise to purchasing our product.

30-Second Report

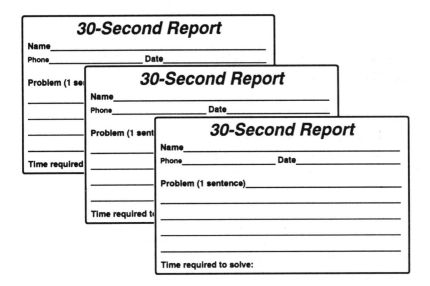

Tracking Systems

The 30-Second Report

The easiest and most universal system for tracking Troubleshooting tasks is the "30-Second Report." Here's the process: Every time we are required to stop everything else we're doing and perform a Troubleshooting task, make a record. Carry or keep available a deck of 3 x 5 cards for this purpose; it helps if the cards are a distinctive color. When we get a call for help, we grab a card and write the date and time, the caller's name and phone number.

After we have solved the problem (or someone else has), we write how long the solution took. It's important to keep it short—a phrase or a sentence is enough. The note only has to have enough information to provoke our own memory about the situation 30 days later. It is intended as a discussion aid, not a written report.

Somewhere visible on a Troubleshooter's desk—or on a wall in the work area—a Troubleshooter should create a place to display completed index cards. The Troubleshooter can arrange this display to separate events that fit expectations (for response time, solution time, first-pass success and manner) from events that, for some reason, fell outside the expectations. This visible collection of cards provides the instant and continuous feedback that Troubleshooters need to assess how current performance compares to the expected results.

The stacks also provide a quick summary of how much Trouble-shooting work is being required every week or month. By observing trends, Troubleshooters can predict roughly how much time they'll need to make available for handling emergencies. This helps them avoid overload and gives them a basis for negotiating with their Role Sets if they need more resources or are also expected to work on Routine and Project tasks.

Note that these records are sometimes kept with a small tape recorder and later transcribed to a broader database. The major drawback of this method, however, is that tape-recorded notes don't give the immediate, on-going, visual data that card stacks do, so taped notes are much less effective as performance feedback.

Checklists and Troubleshooter Handbooks

In Chapter 4, we covered uses for checklists in tracking Routine tasks. Checklists are also a very effective tool for tracking Trouble-shooting tasks. They provide instant reminders about all the issues and steps the Troubleshooter may need to remember (especially when the emergency is an infrequent one) and instant feedback about whether all those items have been addressed.

In fact, the process of preparing emergency checklists is good practice for Troubleshooters. A group of Troubleshooters might meet and make a list of all the kinds of problems that they are called upon to solve. Then the group can sort the problems by type. For each type, the group can design a separate checklist. At the top of each checklist, blanks should be provided for the date, the time at which the call for help was received, the caller's name and phone number, the response time, the source of the problem and the solution time. Most of the rest of each form can be devoted to the checklist itself—specific procedures that the Troubleshooter should remember to follow. The bottom of each form could include space for notes about anything noteworthy that the Troubleshooter encounters.

Multiple copies of these (blank) checklists should be compiled in a binder—*The Troubleshooter's Handbook*—which will serve as a handy reference guide for the most common problems and a storage place for blank record forms. If the list of problem types is long, a Table of Contents should be prepared for the first page of the handbook. The checklists for each problem type also could be color-coded or separated by tabs.

When a problem occurs, the Troubleshooter can simply pull a blank copy of the appropriate checklist from the binder and use it to compile a report. After filling in the blanks and checking off the appropriate steps, the Troubleshooter can put the form in a stack or pin it to a wall, like the 30-Second Reports described on page 133. Each event will get a separate form.

This sort of checklist can provide a more complete record of an event than a 30-Second Report, because it also includes information about the steps taken to solve the problem. When solutions turn out to be inadequate, this sort of record can help pinpoint problems in the Troubleshooter's methods.

Computer Databases

Many Troubleshooters work with computers as their constant companions. Every time Troubleshooters answer the phone or call on a customer, they make notes electronically. They also may be able to use the computer to display an ongoing record of their Troubleshooting performance.

With a little preparation, a special computerized database form can be used in place of 30-Second Report cards or checklists. These records should be designed to display summary data as they are collected—especially the frequency of Troubleshooting events and their average solution time. A special window menu bar or start-up message containing the data can display the information immediately and continuously, so it serves as performance feedback.

Troubleshooters should make a point of reviewing data every month to help uncover patterns in their work.

Remember that if an unpredictable occurs infrequently, it may lend itself to one of the tracking methods used for Projects—Gantt charts and "To-Do" lists. But when the unpredictable appears frequently—whether it's an emergency repair or a Negotiable—performance should be tracked with: 30-Second Reports, Checklists or Computer Databases.

Using Our Database for Permanent Solutions

Analyzing the Data

Troubleshooting data can be analyzed for patterns in a variety of ways. They can help identify the primary sources of repeated problems, the amount of time spent on Troubleshooting tasks and the cycles in which certain problems recur. Each type of analysis is explained below.

Time Spent in Troubleshooting

It's important to discover exactly how much time is being spent on Troubleshooting tasks. Time spent in emergency maintenance affects the cost of processes, and data about this can indicate the economic and other benefits of improving processes. Analyzing time trends can also help Troubleshooters predict (somewhat) the amount of time that they'll need to allow each week for emergencies.

Pareto Analysis

This method of analysis seeks to pinpoint major sources of recurrent problems. We usually find that 80 percent of problems arise from the same 20 percent of possible sources or causes. Troubleshooting data can help identify that 20 percent. Most of the time, to eliminate these major sources, it is necessary either to redesign a process, or to retrain the people who are having (or causing) trouble with a process.

Cycle Analysis—Long-Term Storm Patterns

If Troubleshooters keep their data long enough, they may start to notice cycles in the frequency of certain problems. This information can help pinpoint weaknesses in current Routine processes or can alert the organization to staffing needs.

For example:

◆ A large international bank can predict how many customers will come through each of its several thousand branches during any hour of any day, any week in the year—within 5 percent accuracy. Tellers built the database with 30-Second Reports.

◆ A major fast-food chain can estimate each store's inventory needs for every day of the year with incredible precision—to within one package (eight hamburger buns) at the end of a 2,000-hamburger day. Customers enjoy fresh food because inventory problems were tracked with 30-Second Reports.

Sustaining Expertise for Troubleshooting

The primary resources needed by people who do Troubleshooting and Negotiable tasks are:

◆ access to information;

◆ analytical and prescriptive expertise; and

◆ stress management.

Although everyone in an organization must take these resource issues seriously, they are critical to the survival and effectiveness of people who perform Troubleshooting tasks.

Access to Information

Information technology is completely changing our perceptions of what individuals can accomplish as Troubleshooters. New and expanding electronic databases permit precise, comprehensive answers to many of the questions that Troubleshooters confront. Unfortunately, access to these databases—and authority to act on the information they provide—are not always included in a Troubleshooter's defined role.

Thus, Troubleshooters must become advocates within their organizations for redesigning their roles. The people at the scene of a problem need both information and authority to turn these situations into opportunities for improvement.

Every Troubleshooter should also take the initiative to develop information technology skills. An ability to work with computer networks and databases is rapidly becoming a basic skill for this kind of work.

Finally, Troubleshooters must persuade their organizations to collect and organize the data they gather when they're doing repair work. Only through information-sharing—building and using common databases—will Troubleshooters be able to enrich their performance and contribute to improvements in their organizations' Routine and Project processes.

Expert Programs

One of the best applications of information technology is the *expert program*. This is a type of software that breaks Troubleshooting tasks into a series of questions and procedures, then guides Troubleshooters as they diagnose a problem and prescribe a solution. These programs actually are electronic flowcharts or checklists, and when they're done well, they add thoroughness and efficiency to Troubleshooting that paper forms never achieve.

Examples

Expert programs are used by:

◆ doctors to diagnose illness and prescribe treatment;

◆ auto mechanics to repair cars;

◆ insurance salespeople and financial planners to serve clients; and

◆ human resource practitioners to help employees choose benefits or plan their careers.

Those of us who are Troubleshooters can vastly improve our own services with these tools. We should contribute to the development of these tools to ensure that we are able to use them and advocate their application in our organizations.

Stress Management

As mentioned earlier, Troubleshooting often involves distress. Troubleshooters serve troubled people who are often demanding, quick to blame, slow to learn and rarely forgiving. Emergency conditions are frequently an unpleasant soup of negative emotions.

Thus, it's especially appropriate for Troubleshooters to tend to their own emotional needs through support groups and counseling. Chapter 9 also discusses the "Three A's of Emotional Control"—acknowledging, accepting and acting upon our own emotions—which are essential skills for Troubleshooters.

If we don't learn to take care of ourselves, we won't have the empathy that makes it possible for us to understand and forgive the people with whom we work. Without these abilities, our Troubleshooting will probably never achieve the higher levels of mastery that make us most effective and valuable.

Master Troubleshooters are especially aware of their Role Sets. They must be careful to maintain healthy Role Sets within their own organizations and be able to identify quickly and work with customer Role Sets, as well. In Chapter 1 we examined the dynamics of Role Sets, and the next chapter, on Performance Planning, has much more to say on the subject.

Summary: Serving and Learning at the Edge of Control

Always at the edge of our organization's basic systems is the reality that has not been tamed: new markets and fickle customers, incomprehensibly complex designs, mysteries of physics and chemistry, crime, illness—all the ways the sea of entropy laps at the shores of our tiny island called an organization. Every day, most of us must spend some time rebuilding the seawalls through Troubleshooting and Negotiable tasks.

The work is largely reactive and defensive. It involves quick fixes and temporary stopgaps. Tomorrow, it may have to be done again. And if we're not good at it, we can exhaust ourselves, lose faith in progress and be swept into chaos.

But when we are good at Troubleshooting and Negotiables, we are the first to glimpse new possibilities. Our struggles become more than random reactions. Each response becomes a perception and a memory, and when we reflect upon and analyze these things, our work becomes part of a creative process. We contribute to redesigning our organization's basic systems and actually expand the boundaries of order. New parts of reality move into our understanding, and new responses to problems enlarge the domain in which people can work in harmony.

Like all work, Troubleshooting and Negotiables involve risks and suffering. But perhaps more than other tasks, these can lead to results that make the suffering worthwhile.

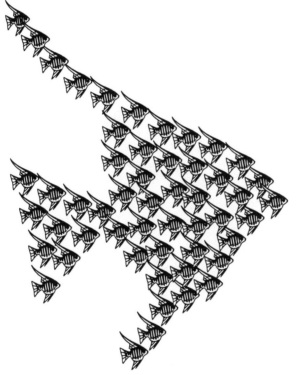

Making Role Sets into Support Systems

Provoking Good Working Relationships with Performance Plans

♦ ♦ ♦ ♦

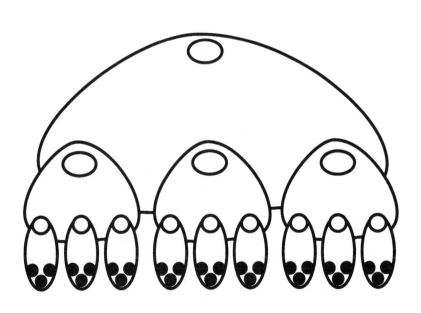

Overview

One-to-one communication—in face-to-face meetings, by phone or in writing—is the most common channel for communicating at work. Often these communications are very brief—just a few words. Occasionally we might write a report instead, or sit down with a colleague for a while and talk at length. The purpose of these work-related communications is usually to clarify expectations, exchange feedback about how things are going and engage in problem solving—i.e., to get or allocate the resources we need to do our jobs.

Much is known about *how* to talk about these things. A few of the current labels for these how-to skills are: *rapport-building, active listening, nonaggressive inquiry and advocacy, probing for underlying assumptions and values, securing enrollment* and *negotiating for win/win agreements.* These skills are all important, but the single most important and helpful thing we can do to ensure effective communication at work is to know *what* to talk about. Whenever we lose sight of the work-related *purpose* of our communications, all the how-to techniques can wind up sounding a bit contrived.

This chapter focuses on what we *should* be talking about—our Performance Plan—a brief statement of the concrete results we intend to produce during the next few months. When we make this statement, we declare our perception of what our working relationships are about—the *purpose* of our relationships with colleagues. Each of us should keep one of these statements ready in our memory at all times and use it many times each day. By focusing our communications at work on these key results, we can put everything else in its proper perspective.

Performance Plans are an especially effective way of keeping everyone informed about what we perceive our own role to be at work. Formulating and advocating a Performance Plan is a key skill for maintaining relationships with the members of our Role Set. If we state our Performance Plans frequently, our Role Sets will come into sharper focus. When our Role Sets and our own key objectives are clearly in focus, alliances become possible, conflict moves into the open where it can be dealt with in a reasonable way and we can ensure that others' expectations of us stay realistic.

Clearly focused work relationships do not come naturally—they don't happen unless we tend to them continually. They aren't static, and they rarely work smoothly all the time. But the most effective way to keep work relationships functioning smoothly and productively is to focus communications on our Performance Plans.

Key Concepts

◆ A Performance Plan is a verbal statement of the few key results we intend to achieve in the next 6 to 12 months. The statement must be:
  – brief;
  – focused on results;
  – specific;
  – attentive to priorities; and
  – comprehensive.
◆ We use Performance Plans to keep roles and expectations clear, especially with members of our Role Sets. Frequent use of these statements is the key to reducing the distress of Role Ambiguity, Role Conflict and Role Overload.

Possible Activities

◆ Draft a Performance Plan.
◆ Test Performance Plans in the "Cocktail" setting.

How Performance Plans Align Our Work with Others

Instant Role Negotiation

The discussion of how to formulate and articulate a Performance Plan begins with a real-life example.

It was my first appointment with Youssef El-Mansy, director of a technology-development facility for Intel, a computer microchip manufacturer based in California's Silicon Valley. (El-Mansy's facility is in Portland, Oregon.) The purpose of our meeting was to set objectives for my consulting work with El-Mansy and his colleagues. I was expecting my usual effort to establish rapport, learn all the buzzwords that might hide problems in the organization and cut through confusion to determine possible solutions to whatever problems El-Mansy identified. Sometimes three or four of these discussions are necessary before the problem-solving work can actually begin.

After a few minutes of small talk, I asked: "What are the key results that must be achieved here during the next 12 months?"

Without a pause, Youssef said: "We're working on four products: A, B, C and D. Product A is in the last stages of development and will be transferred to a manufacturing facility by the end of March. Products B and C are the ones we're focused on developing right now. Product B will be transferred to the manufacturing facilities in Israel and Arizona by July 1. Product C will be manufactured right here when it's ready. If you look out the window, you'll see the new, half-billion-dollar facility we're going to start moving into in June. When we move there, we'll leave this current facility behind as a manufacturing operation to make Product C. Another facility in New Mexico will also make Product C, and we have to make sure that the process gets transferred there properly.

"By the end of this year, we must be fully operational in the new facility here, and we must find ways to cut the production time for Product D by at least six months. We want D ready for transfer to a manufacturing unit by November of next year.

"To get all this done, my staff will have to show some extraordinary cooperation—more than we've ever demonstrated before. That's what I want you to show us how to do."

In less than three minutes, Youssef had stated the whole Performance Plan for the organization he directs and had shown me what my role was to be.

The rest of the hour moved equally efficiently. I probed each project to understand the key players and issues. Youssef and I reviewed the plans for the move to the new facility. We looked at his organizational structure and the system of meetings by which work was being coordinated. After about 55 minutes, I was able to identify which meetings and managers I wanted to start with, and what my objectives were.

Youssef ended the discussion with the comment: "Give me an outline of what we've discussed today. Plan to spend at least two to five days a month here for the next six months. I think a good ongoing measure of your effectiveness will be whether, when I tell my people you're coming, they schedule time with you. Let me warn you, they're awfully busy! Would you be comfortable agreeing that your contract will run for as long as they keep finding it a priority to talk with you?"

I agreed. The result expected of my work was the result expected from everyone else: to get products A through C transferred to manufacturing on time and to reduce the development time for Product D. As long as the members of the management team felt my work contributed significantly to achieving those goals, I had a contract.

I worked with Youssef's team for nine months, and they achieved all their goals. As I learned very quickly, they were an extraordinary team. They were inventing manufacturing processes for the world's most complex microprocessors. They had an incredibly sophisticated manufacturing line and were trying to perfect the processes for four different products—each of which was in an entirely different stage of development. During that year, the team was also moving its work to an entirely new line of equipment in a brand new facility with a lot of new people. And they intended to do it without missing a beat.

Goal Alignment

One of the most obvious contributors to the success of Youssef's team was *goal alignment.* That is the secret to flat, fast, flexible and focused organizational performance. It is not easy to achieve or to maintain. Every person in the system must spend time on it every day—it must be the most talked-about thing in the organization.

At the end of one of my first meetings with Youssef's staff of 14 people, I asked them all to write down what they thought Youssef's Performance Plan to be for the coming year. When they shared their notes with one another, they found that everyone had listed the same set of results. Furthermore, they were in nearly perfect agreement about the relative priority of each result.

As I moved downward in the management structure to the machine operators, I was impressed to find that nearly every one of the 350 employees understood the organization's Performance

Plan, as well. They could also describe their own personal Performance Plans. Like me, they knew where they fit and had chosen to do their parts.

This goal alignment made it very easy for everyone to identify and evaluate opportunities for improvement. We could quickly assess whether or not a suggestion was relevant. And we could determine whether the potential benefits of the suggestions were worth the effort to change. The team's discussions always involved lots of questions, piles of information and plenty of disagreement. But the right people always seemed to be talking about the right things at the right times.

When any decision to change was made, people were unusually quick to alter their roles and behaviors. Motivation never seemed to be a problem. As soon as everyone understood a change as relevant to the goals, people began making it. It seemed *natural*. We were able to achieve some "extraordinary cooperation," to re-use Youssef's phrase.

I've never seen any group reap the benefits of goal alignment except through constant talking. Annual and quarterly reviews of goals may contribute to organizational success, but they are not enough. Goal alignment requires continual discussion. If we don't keep talking about what we're doing together, we're unlikely to make it happen.

My confidence in this statement is supported by more than 30 years of research by those who study organizational behavior. These experts have always noticed that effective managers create an unusual focus of energy in their organizations and that their key behavior is to continually repeat the few major results they plan to achieve in the next 12 to 18 months. Effective managers carry these intended results around on the tips of their tongues. These results are the points around which good managers organize their meetings, their memos, their schedule of appointments, their attention to their mail. A good manager's entire performance will make sense as a focused effort to achieve a few key results.

Because this behavior has appeared so prominently in research, it can be described quite specifically. It has been called by many names—leader expectations, clear goals or objectives, the agenda. I call it "advertising your Performance Plan."

The Essentials of a Good Performance Plan

The qualities of a good Performance Plan have remained the same for at least 30 years. (The importance of articulating a Performance Plan seems to be increasing, however, as we move toward faster, more complex forms of human cooperation.)

A good Performance Plan is:

Simple.

- ◆ It names fewer than seven key results.
- ◆ Its speaker has memorized it, and those who hear it stated often find it easy to remember.
- ◆ It can be described in fewer than three minutes—often in fewer than 90 seconds.
- ◆ When written, a good Performance Plan never covers more than one page.

Results-oriented.

- ◆ It states only what will be accomplished, produced and/or delivered.
- ◆ It is not a list of activities.
- ◆ It does not attempt to describe the *processes* leading to the results.
- ◆ It is not, by itself, a complete plan. (Such plans exist elsewhere in the system.)

Concrete and specific.

- ◆ Results will be observable in some tangible form.
- ◆ The pace and quality expectations for the results are often specified.

Prioritized.

- ◆ Typically, these priorities are described as percentages: for example, 60 percent of the effort will focus on result A; 25 percent on result B; 15 percent on result C.

Comprehensive.

◆ The combined results represent at least 80 percent of what the resources under the speaker's control will be used to accomplish.

◆ The statement includes results to be achieved through both ongoing efforts and efforts to change.

◆ The statement is not merely a list of changes or new projects.

Sample Performance Plans

Following are several Performance Plans. Because they are most important as *verbal behavior* rather than as written documents, they are presented here as people might actually say them. As we read them, we will consider how well they meet the criteria for good Performance Plans. Are they simple? Focused on results? Concrete and specific? Expressed in terms of relative priorities? Comprehensive?

If we were to work with any of these people, would we know right away what the job involved? If we wanted to change something, would we have a clear idea of the issues we'd need to address?

A Customer Service Manager

"This year we anticipate a 20 percent increase in customer calls, and my current staff has to be able to handle that. Making sure that happens is about 40 percent of my job.

"To help that process, I have to make sure that the new information retrieval system is on-line by the end of March. I have to coordinate that with the vendor. I figure that's another 30 percent of this year's effort.

"The last 30 percent of my plan includes three things:

◆ We have to reduce the ratio of customer call-backs from 7 percent to 3 percent.

◆ We've got to learn to answer more of the calls we're transferring up to management—the current amount is running close to 20 percent, and we've got to bring it down to 5 percent.

◆ We've got to learn better ways for dealing with really 'off the wall' customers—the big emotional scenes. The training department is helping me find a course for this."

A Member of the Manager's Customer Service Team

"I'm handling about 80 customer inquiries a week right now; I've got to be doing 100 by this summer. That's at least 80 percent of my goal. Everything else in my plan relates to making sure that happens!

"It won't be easy, because I've got to stop transferring as many calls to management as I have been. I've been transferring about eight a week, and I've got to bring that down to one or two.

"And I've got to get the ones I resolve to stay resolved. I get about five call-backs a week, and that has to come down to not more than two if I'm going to meet my goal of 100 per week. Call-backs really mess things up!"

"We're getting a new computer system to help search the files, and some training to help us cool out the customers who are so mad they can't think straight. I'm going to be doing a lot of learning."

A Fabrication Plant Manager

"The big job is getting the mature products—the ones we've been producing for two years or more—under total quality control. We've been working at this for a year already, but this year our quality has to be zero defects on *all* mature products, so we can continue squeezing out pretty good profit margins. Zero defects on mature products is 40 percent of my plan this year.

"Supporting that goal is another part of my plan—to automate 23 of the sub-processes in manufacturing. That's about 20 percent of my job.

"Another 20 percent is to work with all our materials suppliers to establish 'just-in-time' delivery schedules for all materials we use to make mature products.

"All this adds up to 80 percent, so you can see that mature products are the name of the game for us this year.

"The other 20 percent of the job is to put some heat on the new products team. We've got to reduce the time they're taking to design products, and get them to pay attention to our manufacturing problems earlier. If we can start production at higher levels of quality, we can put new products in the hands of customers much earlier."

An Engineer in the Manager's Fabrication Plant

"I'm called an 'individual contributor,' but I only work alone about 20 percent of the time—that is when I do my reading and writing for the various projects I'm working on.

"I'm on the new-products task force, and that's the most important part of my job for the next several months. By September we're supposed to have the P3 product out the door. That will be the first time we've taken a significant product from idea to customer in fewer than nine months. About 60 percent of my evaluation this year will be based on my work with that Task Force.

"I'm also on two other teams that will be automating certain parts of the production line. One of those teams will finish installing the robots that will move materials from stations B1 through B7 in the manufacturing line by the end of this month. The other team will further automate all the silicon-wafer ovens by the first of June—this will reduce the ovens' operating time by about 30 percent. When these tasks are completed, I'll join a couple new project teams. Projects like these make up the other 40 percent of my job.

"Like everybody else, I will be spending my whole year speeding things up!"

An Equipment Operator in the Fabrication Plant

"I work with two others to load and unload three silicon-wafer ovens. On a good day, we get three loads in and out of each oven. The procedures are very exact—you have to do it perfectly or all hell breaks loose, and the yields drop significantly. We have to get yields of at least 95 percent on each wafer we cook.

"It's been hard to keep up lately—the engineers are making a lot of changes to the equipment. We operators have to learn new procedures nearly every month. But by the end of this year, the modifications will settle down—and then we're supposed to get four loads a day from each oven!"

A Technical Representative (Different Company)

"I take care of my company's equipment in our customer's plant. The customer uses our equipment to make insulation materials—the stuff that goes in the walls and attics of buildings. The customer runs four production lines, 24 hours a day. So I've got to take care of four machines.

"Preventive maintenance is 50 percent of my job—my machines must perform at the levels of precision and durability specified in our contract. Half of my preventive maintenance work involves training operators and supervisors; the other half involves working directly on the machines.

"Dealing with emergencies is another 30 percent of my job. If one of our machines goes down—any time of day or night—I have to be on-site, looking cheerful and diagnosing the problem, within 15 minutes. In 80 percent of cases, I'm supposed to bring the machine back on-line in less than an hour.

"If, in my first 30 minutes on-site, it becomes clear that I won't be able to solve the problem in an hour, I have to tell the production-line supervisor and the shift manager right away. I need to give them a reliable estimate of how long the repair will take, then call for a senior technician and any necessary repair parts. The parts and senior tech are supposed to be here immediately, so that we can fix even serious problems within two hours, 99 percent of the time.

"The final 20 percent of my job is to pass tests twice a year to prove I paid attention during training sessions.

"Happy me, happy machines, happy customers—that's it—just one big happy job."

A Software Engineer (Different Company)

"Some engineers work on major projects, and it's pretty easy for them to say what they'll be doing this year. But I'm a maintenance engineer—I'm responsible for making sure the design team for Product 5 has software tools that work properly. The tools are new, and we're de-bugging them as we go.

"My job is all service-on-demand—emergencies!

"The problems are small stuff 80 percent of the time; I can fix them permanently in less than eight hours. I'll probably make about 300 of those repairs this year—somewhat fewer than two a day.

"The rest of the time, I'll be dealing with problems that are real snakes—who knows how they'll squirm and slither? They usually become short-term redesign projects—I make a quick fix and then set about finding a lasting solution. I have to keep these projects on the 'back burner' while I respond to emergencies. All I can do about estimating solution times for those projects is to commit myself to a goal when the problem is first discovered."

Park Maintenance Supervisor

"I've got 12 full-time employees and 7 contractors to maintain 13 parks. Money's scarce, so we're just doing the basics and trying to find ways to cut costs.

- ◆ Fifteen percent of the job is to keep the grass green and mowed.
- ◆ Fifteen percent of the job is to keep the trees healthy and pick up the fallen leaves.
- ◆ Fifteen percent of the job is to pick up the garbage.
- ◆ Fifteen percent of the job is to maintain recreational areas— baseball diamonds, soccer fields, tennis courts, picnic areas. We're collecting user fees for all of these now.
- ◆ Thirty percent of the job is to keep the restrooms clean and operational. (That's tough these days—a lot of homeless people are practically camping in our restrooms.)
- ◆ Five percent of our effort is to replace high-maintenance growth (flowers, exotic plants, shrubs and trees) with low-maintenance growth.
- ◆ And that leaves just five percent for maintaining a few flower beds.

"That tells you where all the flowers have gone."

A Gardener Contracting with the Parks Department
"I just mow lawns. I have 12 different lawns in 3 different parks. They're all bigger than football fields, and they wind all over the place, almost like golf courses. I mow each one roughly every two weeks.

"Each lawn is a little different, and I used to get hassled about whether I was doing them right—or fast enough. But I fixed that. I made a checklist for each lawn and set a deadline for getting each one done. The checklist even includes time for equipment maintenance. I got the boss to agree.

"Now everybody knows we're doing the mowing faster and better and cheaper than ever. You show me a lawn; I'll tell you exactly how and when it will be done."

Advocating Our Performance Plans To Protect Ourselves from Role Ambiguity, Conflict and Overload

The most important benefit of a Performance Plan is that it helps keep Role-Set relationships healthy. As mentioned in Chapter 1, our Role Set is composed of three to eight people who depend on our performance and influence our behavior by offering rewards or punishments when we satisfy or disappoint their expectations.

The three pathologies that occur in Role Sets are: *Role Ambiguity,* when expectations for the focal person's performance are unclear; *Role Conflict,* when the expectations are flatly contradictory; and *Role Overload,* when the expectations are simply impossible to meet. Each of these pathologies causes specific kinds of emotional and physical harm in the focal person. These pathologies also create distrust in the relationships. To maintain our individual health and our team effectiveness, we must combat these pathologies by moving them into the open where we can see them and deal with them reasonably. Performance Plans are tools that we can use toward that end.

Pathology		*Strategy*
Instead of Ambiguity	—>	Clear Expectations
Instead of Conflict	—>	Aligned Expectations
Instead of Overload	—>	Realistic Expectations

We might think that the easiest way to clear up a problem is to go to the members of our Role Set and ask them what they want. But many people who try this approach run into problems. First, it isn't always easy to know who the members of our Role Set are. Second, the people who *are* in our Role Set might not know what they really want from us. They might not have thought it through very carefully. They might just be reacting negatively toward us whenever they happen to feel disappointed. And they might feel even *more* disappointed when we start asking questions; they might think we're trying to blame them for something or to "pick a fight." Then they might start reacting with more punishment.

It's much more constructive for us to *advocate our roles rather than to inquire about them.*

And the best way to advocate our role is to have a clear Performance Plan, which will give others a clear snapshot of what we understand our own role to be. In other words: start telling everybody what we think we're supposed to be doing. We must develop and memorize our own Performance Plans and start announcing them to anyone who could possibly be affected by our effort to achieve them. And we can't just do this once in awhile; we must keep it up all the time.

This behavior will cause things to happen all around us—it will provoke others to respond. Things will begin to change, including our Performance Plans—so we'll need to revise them and teach our Plans to everyone all over again. Our announcements of our own Performance Plans will provoke one of three responses in our audience: *alliance, apathy or resistance.*

Alliance Responses

Alliance, of course, is the kind of response we're hoping for. We say, "This is what I intend to accomplish during the next 12 months: X, Y and Z." The other person responds, "Right on! That's what I thought you were going to do. That's what I need for you to do."

When we get an alliance response, the next step is to *secure the alliance with a mutual action plan.* We must begin to explore how we can cooperate to achieve the results we just specified in our Performance Plan. Say, "Great—let's talk about what we both need to do to make it happen." It's important to take this step, so we can test whether other people's responses are really an alliance, or they just look like one on the surface. If other people are truly allies, they will show how they are currently cooperating, or how they can cooperate. They will reinforce the approval message with concrete action.

If apparent allies don't join in the action-planning, however, they are probably just being polite, which means they're really making an apathy response.

Apathy Responses

Most of us don't particularly like apathetic responses to our Performance Plans. We're usually fairly committed to our Plans and see them as reasonable and respectable. When someone else responds with glazed, bored eyes or a polite smile-off, we're usually a little offended. But there's good news in those glazed eyes and polite smiles: anyone who hears our whole Performance Plan and responds with genuine apathy is not a member of our Role Set, and we don't need to worry about what they think of our performance.

By definition (and psychological reality), the members of our Role Set see themselves as depending on our performance. They always pay attention when they find out what we're planning to do, and they always respond with either alliance or resistance, which we'll discuss in a moment. So apathy responses lead us to an important discovery: these tuned-out people are not in our Role Set!

This is valuable information, because it takes a lot of time and energy to maintain good relations with the members of our Role Set. We may not like everyone in our Role Set, but we must know who they are, and we must understand each of them well enough to avoid distress and job failure. No human is able to manage very many of these relationships at once—they require too much energy and attention. So an important self-management skill is to find out who our Role Set members are and save our energy for them.

When we receive an apathy response, the next step is to be *polite*. No matter how shocked or offended we feel about someone's apathy, it's important to shift the conversation to small talk by asking an open-ended question, then finding an excuse to move away. We might ask how the people's children are, how they liked yesterday's ballgame, how they are celebrating an upcoming holiday, where they grew up, etc. We shouldn't stand chatting longer than seven minutes. If we stand around longer than that, people start feeling pressure to get serious about something—and we don't need to get serious with these people. A polite exit will be appreciated: We've got to prepare for a meeting; we're expecting a phone call; our electronic mail is stacked up.

A polite response keeps doors open for a future relationship. Although these apathetic people aren't in our Role Set now, they may be later. There's no point in starting off on a bad note. And we don't have to be offended by the apathy—it has nothing to do with our value as a person, or with the value of our Plan. It simply means that our plan and theirs are irrelevant to each other at the moment. We can accept this and move on to other, more crucial relationships.

But what if we suspect the apathy response is just a cover for resistance? Should we still just let the moment pass politely? Probably. But we can continue advocating our Plan to this person in the future—and try it in different settings. When we think that people's behavior signals obvious resistance, we can begin negotiating a resolution to the conflict.

What if the person making an apathetic response is our boss? This is not common, but it does happen. Again, we'll have to pass the moment politely and give ourselves some time to think the situation over. Why doesn't our boss depend on our performance?

Do we understand the boss's Performance Plan? Do we think we're significantly related to that Plan? If so, we can test again with further announcements of our Performance Plan. If there's still "nobody home," we might have to set up a meeting to renegotiate our Plan.

There are occasions, however, when it's fine to discover that our boss is not in our Role Set. If we don't depend on our boss to get the resources we need to perform our role, and other significant people are allied with us on the Plan, then we can just go ahead with it. Some accident or warp may have occurred in the organization's formal structure, but correcting it may not be important.

Resistance Responses

Announcements of our Performance Plan might also provoke resistance—one of the people in our Role Set might respond, "What?! That's not right. I don't want you to do that. Stop it!"

Most of us shy away from conflict—it seems dangerous, so we try to avoid provoking this response. Some of us hope that if we ignore conflict, it will go away. But it won't.

There is simply no way for human beings to work in groups without conflict. We disagree about goals, about processes and about the meaning of feedback we get from customers. We also compete for the organization's limited resources.

If we ignore these realities, they can only be expressed through covert methods—passive resistance, character assassination, sabotage and ambush. These covert forms of conflict are the most distressing and dangerous—they create suspicion in the work group, because they ferment in darkness and then erupt unexpectedly.

The only way to make conflict safe and functional is to drive it into the open—convert it to overt conflict—the sooner the better. It is always easier to deal with conflict in its early stages before it gets too complex and emotionally charged.

Advocating one's Performance Plan drives conflict into the open. This at least creates an opportunity for it to be dealt with reasonably. Most of the time, when conflict is in the open, people prefer a reasonable resolution through negotiation—it is a risk very much worth taking. The next step is to negotiate.

We start by inquiring: What's wrong with my intentions? What's the basis of our misunderstanding or disagreement? What plan are we trying to accomplish that differs from theirs? How can we at least get out of each other's way? Is there anything we can do that might make us helpful to each other?

We first *seek to understand and be understood.* We don't try to leverage or sell our way to agreement, and we don't let the other person do that to us, either. Sooner or later, we'll arrive at a common perception of how our work relates to the organization's purpose and goals. Those goals are the basis for our cooperation, and we can plan from there.

Or perhaps we'll discover that we're working from fundamentally different assumptions about our organization. In that case, we can push our conflict upward in the organization until a decision clarifies the situation. These are the two options in which cooperation is guided by reason.

Of course, there are less reasonable organizations in which conflict always means a win-lose power game. Such organizations are simply doomed to all the distress and poor performance that arise from covert conflict. Most people cannot and will not play in a game where every acknowledgment of conflict is an invitation to duel. We find other ways to protect ourselves from the bullies who seem to thrive on such games: we leave, get sick, avoid meeting with them or practice forms of passive resistance when we have to be around them. We also form "underground" alliances, more or less consciously, that cause the bullies to fail.

To negotiate in good faith requires a willingness to compromise—and willingness to change. To resolve a conflict, we may need to change our Performance Plans: drop some elements altogether, scale them down or rearrange their priority. We may need to add other elements. Cooperation doesn't necessarily mean marching in lockstep. It can, however, braid together many individual, zig-zagging paths toward our common purpose, instead of just combing us into straight, parallel lines.

When our negotiations lead to changes in our Performance Plans, we'll need to announce the new Plans to everyone again. We'll find ourselves talking about our Plans a lot. That's why we need to keep the Plans simple enough that we can explain them quickly and specific and comprehensive enough to make our intentions clear.

Build a Realistic Plan

When negotiating with a person who resists our Plan, *or* when action-planning with an ally, we might discover that the other person expects more from us than we expect to deliver. That calls for a frank exploration of the available resources.

Do we have the equipment, supplies, skills, information, authority and cooperation necessary to meet the higher expectations? It's always a good idea to challenge our own assumptions about what is possible. Others have a right to expect us to make genuine efforts to think creatively about how we use our resources so that we can improve efficiency and the quality of our results.

We also owe it to ourselves and our colleagues to be realistic. When we really can't see any way to achieve the higher expectations, we have to say so. Gambling on slim probabilities or praying for miracles is not usually in the best interests of cooperation.

It's amazing how often we get emotionally blackmailed into attempting the impossible. We get pumped up with enthusiasm and commit to working permanently at peak levels. Or we succumb to flattery and pride and start thinking of ourselves as superhuman. Once we have deluded ourselves, it is easy to start exploiting our colleagues in the same way: "I'm not asking them to do anything I don't do myself."

There aren't any superhumans. If we try to work all the time at peak levels of performance, we will burn out. Fatigue leads to mental escapism, depression, substance abuse and even suicide.

It is essential that we respect ourselves—and others—as ordinary human beings. Skills can improve; new methods can make higher performance a permanent reality; rearranged priorities may enable us to improve some performances while sacrificing others. For short periods, sheer effort can yield higher results. These are the ways that ordinary human beings work smarter. When the only way to meet higher expectations is to work harder all the time, the expectations are unrealistic. We cannot meet them *and* sustain the longevity and quality of our lives. We owe it to ourselves and our colleagues to negotiate a different set of expectations.

Advocating a Performance Plan makes things happen. It gets us talking about the right things with the right people at the right times. It helps us clarify what we need to do. It clarifies for others what we are doing. After a while, we'll find that we have more allies and fewer worries about resistors. And we'll waste less time on people and issues that aren't relevant to the results of our work.

People will come to us when they see opportunities or significant problems. They will stay away when they know that we're not the right ones to help them achieve their own plans. When all the members of a team have clear and appropriate plans, their relationships with one another are more polite and less stressed. Individual members may not love one another, but they probably won't go out of their way to hurt one another, either. It's a better way to work.

The only thing that prevents most of us from getting started is that we don't quite know how to push all our work into a Performance Plan statement. Chapters 4 to 6, which covered Breakthrough Systems for Routine, Project, and Unpredictable tasks, offer many suggestions about how to state expectations. Below are additional exercises that can help.

Your Turn: Writing Your Own Performance Plan

Steps to Take

1. On a blank page, list all the activities included in your job and the jobs of people you manage.

2. Review the list and cross out any activities directly related to managerial work: i.e., those aimed at clarifying expectations, providing performance feedback or acquiring resources. Management activity always relates to the *processes* of work, not the results. Performance Plans are only about results. If you're a designated "manager," your Plan should summarize the results to be achieved by people who report directly to you. (See figure on page 162.)

3. Name the outputs for all the activities remaining on the list.

4. This list is the raw material for your Performance Plan. Describe the outputs so they meet the criteria of the figure on page 163.

Separating Results from Management Activities

Results	Management Activities
Market analyzed	Budgeting
Product designed	Writing / reviewing reports
Widget produced	Holding meetings
Maintenance completed	Coaching and counseling
Sales orders taken	Disciplining
Service provided	Appraising performance
Proprietary rights protected	Setting compensation
Expense accounts audited	

The Cocktail Party

Instead of thinking alone about your Performance Plan, you may prefer to develop it with members of your work group. One fun and useful method for doing this is a "cocktail party." The "party" and discussions take about an hour altogether. At the end of the hour, most members of the team will have a good start on the habit of announcing their Performance Plans. Changes will begin happening immediately—roles will become clearer and negotiations about them may get underway. New opportunities for cooperation are usually discovered.

Private Brainstorm

This step ensures that all team members can say their Performance Plans. The best method is to give each member 10 minutes alone to write a first draft. Since most of us have work activities on our minds anyway, it only takes about 10 minutes for most of us to make this list of results.

Performance Plan Checklist

❏	**Simple and emphatic?** • Less than seven statements? • Easily memorized? • Whole plan said in less than three minutes?
❏	**Stated in terms of *results*?**
❏	**Specific?** • Describes concrete Outputs? • Describes Outputs in terms of pace and quality?
❏	**Priorities assigned to each result?** • Spreads 100 points among the results?
❏	**Comprehensive?** • Covers at least 80 percent of the responsibilities? • Covers both changes to be made and activities to remain constant?

First Test

Next, each member pairs up with another member, and they take turns (five minutes each should be enough) saying and listening to each other's Performance Plans. The partners can suggest changes that might help each other's Performance Plans match the checklist summary provided here (or refer to the full description on pages 149-150). Copies of the checklist can be passed out to each pair or displayed on a wall for easy reference.

The Party

Next is the "cocktail party." Everyone stands up and remains standing in a relatively small area for 10 minutes. A designated timekeeper rings a bell to start the "party," and each participant turns to one other person. The pairs take turns saying their Performance Plans to each other. Listeners may ask questions to clarify their understanding of their partners' Plans, but listeners shouldn't use these minutes to suggest changes in the Plans. After three minutes, the timekeeper rings the bell again, and people form new pairs and repeat their Plans to their new partners. Three minutes later the bell rings once more, and everyone changes partners for the third and final round.

Private Reflections

Participants then sit down for five minutes and work alone, making a few notes in response to the following questions:

- ◆ Whose Plans, and what parts of their Plans, do you remember?
- ◆ How did the way you stated your Plan change from Round 1 to Round 3?
- ◆ What responses did you get to your Plan: alliance, resistance or apathy?

The Feedback Party

After reflection, participants return to the cocktail party setting for another five minutes and tell their former partners what they remember about their Plans. (You may want to use a timekeeper again, but usually participants can manage their own time for this task.)

More Private Reflections

After this feedback round, participants take a minute alone to make notes in response to this question: How (if at all) have these last five minutes caused you to change your mind about the responses your Plan is provoking?

Final Discussion

The last step is to hold a 20-minute group discussion, in which everyone can share the notes they've made.

Summary: Keep Talking

The next chapter has more specific things to say about teamwork and the use of Performance Plans in work groups. The point to remember is: Keep talking together about your Plans and your progress toward their fulfillment. Nothing contributes more to healthy, effective work relationships than frequent repetition of our expectations for ourselves and one another.

Our working relationships will be tested repeatedly as our work becomes more complicated, as the demands for speed increase and as changes occur. Unless we are deliberate and skillful about discussing our roles, we may find ourselves experiencing a great deal of distress. Advocating a Performance Plan is a very effective way to start this discussion and continue it.

If we are to achieve the first and most important requirement of the Breakthrough System—clear expectations—we must use a Performance Plan to manage our Role Set. Each of us should "wear" our Performance Plans like bright orange life vests. Onboard our organizations, conditions are no longer safe without them.

Using Meetings To Align Work and Exercise Power

◆ ◆ ◆ ◆

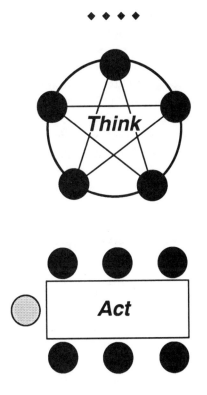

Overview

Many people think that they're already spending too much time in meetings and may roll their eyes at the futility of accomplishing anything significant in them. The problem is that very few people really understand the proper function of meetings and don't know how to run them effectively. Clearly, just gathering people in a room doesn't do the trick. But meetings are critical tools for coordinating group work, especially as work becomes more complex, as information technology speeds the pace of competition and as change becomes continuous. It's essential to use meetings well. We can't afford to let them be a waste of time.

The trouble with most meetings is that they are *nominal groups*—groups in name only. These groups don't actually accomplish much while they're together. The meetings are not set up to take full advantage of the group's intelligence or problem-solving abilities. And most of the people who attend don't participate in ways that influence decisions and determine how the organization will use its resources. Instead, such meetings are little more than occasions for passive listening. Participants aren't even required to understand the activities being described, let alone influence them. We usually attend such meetings, boring as they are, only because the organization's social etiquette requires us to do so.

Another reason we might attend is to make sure that nobody is getting in our way—doing things that we want to do ourselves or demanding resources that we want or need. In that case, the meeting isn't just about disseminating information, it's about ensuring that we don't need one another. We attend such meetings to secure our ability to act autonomously. The group may accomplish some minimal form of coordination, but essentially, the members are trying to avoid one another.

Nominal groups may look like groups, but they don't do group work. Group work involves thinking together and making commitments to cooperative action. When groups really *work* together, the members teach one another and learn from one another. They actively coordinate their efforts, and by sharing information and authority, the group can use its resources more intelligently and efficiently than the individual members could. In today's business environment, that's a survival advantage.

Essentially, there are two kinds of meetings in which group work can actually be done well: *Regular Meetings* and *Task Forces.* If they're functioning properly, Regular Meetings are the place where groups *act*—they process information to *make decisions* about how the organization will use its resources. Regular Meetings are the places where groups exercise their formal authority, their ability to control resources and focus their power to accomplish intended results. Regular Meetings also reflect and create the organization's culture and politics. They are a permanent fixture in the organization's structure.

Task Forces, on the other hand, *think*—they don't decide. They are *temporary* tools for thinking carefully about a complex matter before an organization commits itself to any action. A Task Force is a gathering of relevant experts inside and outside the organization, whose charter is to learn all they can about the issue at hand and recommend a course of action. In addition to workers, a Task Force may include appropriate customers, suppliers, vendors or consultants. Some members may participate in just a few of the meetings. When it has finished its thinking or problem-solving task, the Task Force probably will bring its discoveries and its recommendations to the rest of the organization through Regular Meetings, where actual decisions can be made. Task Forces thus prepare Regular Meetings for intelligent action.

We need to ensure that our meetings aren't merely nominal groups. We must make our organizations' Regular Meetings and Task Forces scenes for genuine group work. Group work will knit our organizations together and build us into an intelligent, committed work force.

Key Concepts

◆ Most meetings are "nominal groups." People in them sit together but don't do genuine group work. Nominal groups are generally a boring waste of time.

◆ When conducted well, two kinds of meetings make effective use of group intelligence and power:

1. Regular Meetings make decisions about how to use an organization's resources. They exercise formal authority.

2. Task Forces *think* for the organization rather than act. They recommend solutions, decisions and plans to Regular Meetings.

♦ Organizations become unusually smart, focused, flexible and fast when we understand and participate actively in these two forms of group work.

Possible Activities

♦ Agree on ways to eliminate nominal groups and start improving the processes in Regular Meetings and Task Forces.

♦ Present, align and take group responsibility for helping all the members of the team achieve their Performance Plans.

We Can't Go On Meeting Like This— Nominal Groups

How Did Our Meetings Get So Bad?

For hundreds of years, the coordination of work has been considered the specialty of management. The assumption has been that work should be broken into a lot of tiny pieces—jobs—and distributed to individuals who will do exactly what the job definition says—no less, no more. This has been considered necessary because most workers have been seen as somewhat simple-minded—incapable of dealing with complexity or responsibility. Smarter and more responsible people, "managers," have been expected to take care of coordinating the simple jobs. This assumption operated in Guild societies, which required craft workers to undergo long apprenticeships, and it continues to operate in industrial societies, where people do repetitive jobs on assembly lines.

Most coordination has been handled through one-on-one communications, in either spoken or written form. In hierarchical systems the world over, the rule is: communication must flow top-down, through *official channels*.

As organizations have grown larger, monopolizing supplies and markets to gain control of costs, prices and the economic advantages of large-scale operations, the strains on official channels of communication have increased. Many forms of organizational structure and practice have been invented to deal with this strain. The result is bureaucracy, and one of bureaucracy's most prominent features is meetings.

The idea has been that more can be communicated if lots of people are gathered together and given many messages at once. These meetings usually are one-way efforts to disseminate information—especially directives. The standard format is that an "official channel" presents information and then may or may not give the audience a chance to ask clarifying questions. Each member of the audience is expected to figure out which messages are relevant to his or her job and how those messages should affect personal performance. If after such a meeting people are found violating one of the directives, they can't plead ignorance as an excuse.

In both theory and in practice, this system has worked—sort of. Wars have been won, taxes collected, systems of transportation built, raw materials collected, products distributed, profits made, new databases assembled, learning perpetuated, and more and more people enfranchised as members of the middle and upper classes.

As organizations have grown, however, more and more information has been poured down the mountain of hierarchy into little pools called meetings. And audiences have spent an enormous amount of time filtering this flood of information for the few messages that are relevant to their particular jobs. In such meetings, it's usually important to appear to be listening, but in fact, most people actually find doodling to be a more compelling activity.

This sort of meeting, where individual bodies sit together but their minds work alone (if at all), is called a nominal group. Just as jobs are compartmentalized in a bureaucracy, so minds are compartmentalized in nominal groups. Neither the people talking nor the people listening learn very much. If a decision is made in such a meeting, it is usually made by an individual, with little influence from any of the others. In fact, no group work is being accomplished at all. It may look like a group, but in fact the members are just sitting in the same room, doing their own things or nothing at all.

The history of meetings has been largely a history of nominal groups. Bureaucracy hasn't required anything more. Therefore, most of our expectations and habits concerning meetings are appropriate only for nominal groups. Today, however, something more is required of us—bureaucratic, top-down, hierarchical systems are not fast, flexible or smart enough to compete or excel.

Let's Meet To Think and Decide

New information technology—computers and software—is changing assumptions about how people can work. Faster, more precise performance is possible, and the cost of quality products and services is plummeting. As costs drop, the products and services fall within the reach of vastly larger markets all over the world. Huge amounts of work are necessary to serve those new markets.

To get all the work done, jobs are being redesigned: i.e., combined and enlarged. Individual workers control much larger portions of their organizations' resources and manage those resources with computerized equipment. Machines handle more and more of the highly specialized or repetitive tasks, so each person can now do jobs that once required hundreds of people. Instead of focusing narrowly on specialized skills, workers are being required to act more as generalists, and to evaluate products and processes from a much broader perspective—the perspective that was once limited to "managers" at the upper levels of a hierarchy. Individuals can no longer succeed, for example, by focusing on just one bolt of the automobile being built, or one section of the insurance application being completed. Instead, we must be able to evaluate the car's entire front end or the client's total insurability. The sheer volume of work, the cost of materials involved and the potential market-value of products and services also require each worker to be responsible for ensuring that jobs are done right the first time, with as little waste as possible.

Jobs enlarge still further when individuals work together in teams. And time pressures increase, because the team depends on each person's ability to handle a share of the workload according to the team's schedule.

Organizations that try to do enlarged jobs in the old, compartmentalized, bureaucratic way can waste their resources very quickly—sometimes several million dollars' worth every minute. Today, an organization's ability to improve the quality, speed and cost of its products and services depends on its skill at integrating jobs and fostering powerful cooperation among teams. Bureaucratic hierarchy with its minutely defined jobs is dead.

Goals, standards and schedules must be set and monitored by teams working collaboratively. Problems must be shared earlier so that others can at least make schedule adjustments and perhaps help with solutions as well. Tools and processes must be designed so that workers can transition smoothly from one to another and processes conducted in parallel can be integrated seamlessly.

Individuals working in teams must learn to share and process information better and faster. No one has time anymore to waste in nominal groups, waiting for relevant information to emerge from a flood of irrelevancies. Organizations can't afford to have people passively waiting to be told what to do. Teams must learn to run their own meetings more effectively and to coordinate their work with other teams. Individuals must go to meetings prepared to teach and learn what they and their colleagues are doing. Each of us must be ready to take action, to participate in making team decisions and commitments.

Meetings can no longer be opportunities for doodling and inattention; they must be places where teams do genuine group work—identifying and solving problems, spotting opportunities and making quick adjustments, removing roadblocks and bottle-necks and celebrating success. Two distinct types of meetings facilitate this group work—Regular Meetings and Task Forces—and teams must learn to conduct both types well.

Two Kinds of Meetings

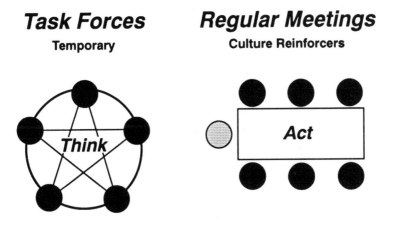

Task Forces
Temporary

Think

Regular Meetings
Culture Reinforcers

Act

In powerful Regular Meetings, groups *act* together and exercise formal authority; they decide how to use the resources under their command. In powerful Task Forces, groups *think;* they analyze complex problems or decisions and make recommendations. Usually, these recommendations are acted upon in Regular Meetings.

Regular Meetings—Exercising Formal Authority

Regular Meetings are the ones held most frequently in effective organizations. They are the on-going centers of intelligence that monitor and regulate an organization's day-to-day life. Each group or team meets regularly (e.g., once a week) to decide how it will use the portion of organizational resources it controls. If the team is composed of front-line workers, the meetings focus on ensuring that their equipment, materials and skills serve their customers well. If the group is composed of managers, the meetings focus on coordinating all the resources that the managers' subordinates control.

The group, of course, is a higher authority than any of its members. Usually the group's authority is represented in the person of its leader. But in an effective, nonbureaucratic organization, group members are expected—in fact required—to *participate* in exercising the leader's authority. If the group members don't understand this clearly, their meetings will soon degenerate into nominal groups, and they will sit passively while the leader tells them what to do.

The difference between a bureaucratic culture and a nonbureaucratic culture can be seen clearly in the *operations review* portion of any group's periodic staff meeting. In a bureaucratic organization, the meeting is a nominal group, and communications are basically a series of one-to-one discussions between the leader and each of the other members in turn. The participants each explain what they are doing with their portions of the group resources, and the leader is the only person who seems genuinely interested in what everyone has to say. The leader is the one who asks questions, makes suggestions, criticizes or congratulates others. Each person is facing the rear of the boat and assumes responsibility only for "pulling his or her own oar"—and only "the boss" worries about where the boat goes. Under those assumptions, group work stops—and the meetings grind along in all their stupidity and boredom.

When a group meets to review its operations in a nonbureaucratic culture, every member thoroughly understands and evaluates every other member's report, including the leader's. All the members invest serious attention in one another's work—not just for their own education, but because they know that their personal success depends on their team members' performances. The team's minds all focus on ensuring that group goals and priorities are commonly understood, that everyone is acting according to the group plans, that problems are being identified and solved, that opportunities are being fully exploited, that all resources are being intelligently employed and that everyone under the team's authority is learning and growing more competent. All members of the team sit facing forward in the boat, and chatter as they paddle to make sure the boat is on course. They know that unless they take responsibility for the whole boat, everyone in the boat is likely to hit a rock and sink.

When we are in nonbureaucratic cultures, we merge individual and team success. No one can afford to let teammates slack off or fail—their failures are our own. We must be ready to assist one another; we must also insist that everyone perform. Being supportive must not be interpreted as politely ignoring each other's poor performance. To respect each other must include expecting each other to perform well and explicitly identifying and working on each other's problems. As a group, we must decide whether the team is succeeding or not, and whether individual performances merit special recognition or corrective action. We must make these decisions together—openly—where everyone can be sure the process is well-informed and fair.

As soon as each of us takes this kind of responsibility for our team's work, our organizations will show extraordinary intelligence, flexibility and speed—much more so than in any other organizational culture. A nonbureaucratic management system—sometimes called *networked management*—offers a significant competitive edge (where this is relevant) and a reliable means for providing quality products and services. Effective meetings are the engines of that system.

Four Kinds of Action for Regular Meetings

Once we understand the authority that we are expected to exercise in Regular Meetings, it becomes obvious that we must go prepared. We need to know the meeting agenda ahead of time, so that we can perform our role responsibly.

The agenda of any Regular Meeting should include up to four basic types of business: *Pass-Downs, Operations Review, Recommendations Review* and *News.* Each of these elements requires collaborative group work, and each requires *action.* In fact, *every* item on a Regular Meeting agenda must be "actionable." If the group can't do anything with or about an agenda item, the group shouldn't waste time on it during the meeting.

Pass-Downs are decisions that a higher-level group has made and sent to subordinate groups to receive their commitments. Usually these items first emerge when lower-level groups raise questions or identify issues that require a higher group's action. Members of various lower-level groups may get involved in preparing information or making recommendations to the higher-level group. Sooner or later, the higher-level group has the information it feels it needs, makes a decision and passes it back to the lower-level groups, where people must understand and implement it. So when a group's Regular meeting agenda includes Pass-Downs, the *action* the team must take on those items is *commitment.* All the members of the group promise to use the resources under their control according to the requirements of the Pass-Down. This promise may require the group to stop something it's doing, to start doing something new, to emphasize different parts of its current performance or to continue doing just what it has been doing.

The **Operations Review** is an ongoing act of group performance evaluation that determines how the group can make the best possible use of the resources it controls. The action groups take during an Operations Review is deciding how resources should be allocated or shifted—how they will manage their own performance and productivity. Team members must prepare constantly for their Operations Reviews—not just by being able to explain their individual contributions to the group effort, but also by understanding what *every other* individual in the group contributes. This is how groups gain a "big picture" understanding of their role in an organization, how they identify problems and solutions quickly and how they know what to adjust as conditions change. It literally means that the teammates must teach and study the tasks and technologies of one another's jobs and outputs. They must ask one another for articles, texts and tutoring and attend problem-solving sessions where key technologies are discussed and applied.

In a **Recommendation Review,** the group's action will be to accept, reject or take corrective action on a recommendation. Usually the recommendation is no surprise, because it has come from some source the group consulted—a Task Force it chartered, a staff person it asked for an opinion or an external vendor or consultant the group hired. Before the Regular Meeting at which the recommendation is reviewed, all members of the group must be sure they understand the thinking behind the recommendation. Informally, group members might ask the recommender questions or offer opinions, to see that their concerns are fully addressed. When the decisive meeting date arrives, the group must examine whether the recommender has carefully collected and analyzed an appropriate body of data, has considered all relevant alternatives and has arrived at the recommendation in a reasonable way. If the group is satisfied by the quality of thinking behind the recommendation, it should then consider the recommendation in relation to its other priorities and decide what to implement. This is the process by which the group should make most major changes in its operations.

The **News** is just that—what's new; what's changing? The purpose of news is to remind the group of changes that may affect its work. News helps the group stay coordinated when members stop or start doing a task or procedure, for example, or when someone discovers conditions that might cause members' work to change. News is an early-warning system important for cooperation. But the only action a News item may require is for the group to keep it in mind. And if it seems boring, long-winded or irrelevant to many members of the group, their minds may go passive. So it's important to keep news announcements succinct and crisp—a headline of around 13 words is a good rule of thumb. Usually, the announcer shouldn't bother detailing the "who, what, where, when and how" unless the group asks. If news announcers discipline themselves in this way, a group of 14 can easily get through all the news in about 10 minutes.

Every person on the team must commit to showing up at every meeting prepared to take action on every agenda item. Anything less is a waste of the group's time and an abdication of its authority. Meetings can be long or short, as long the group's thinking leads to action. When there is no action to take, even a short meeting becomes boring and a waste.

The Basic Process for Taking Action

Regular Meeting agendas usually include three to ten items requiring separate decisions or actions, although they can include many more. The basic process for reaching each decision, however, will involve the same four steps: *Presentation, Review, Decision* and *Commissioning*.

Regular Meeting Basic Process

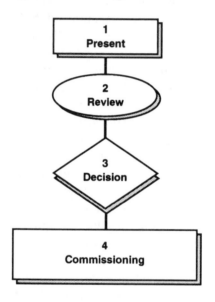

Presentation

The Pass-Down, Operations Report, Recommendation or News Item will be delivered by a group member or a visitor to the meeting. Each presentation should begin with its conclusion—a statement of the action the group is being asked to take. If group members know this first, they can listen more intelligently and see whether the path to the conclusion is reasonable, direct and efficient. Groups should require presenters to be succinct. All they really need to do is lay out:

◆ the *issues* that have been considered;

◆ the *need* for group action; and

◆ a *forecast* of negative and positive consequences that the action is likely to bring.

Review

The longest part of the process is usually the Review. During this time, the group members probe the logic of the presentation, the quality of its data and the appropriateness of the requested action, given the group's goals, priorities and plans. The group must identify and evaluate how the presentation might cause the group to deviate from its plans or change its use of resources. The group must also consider any alternative actions it could take. When the group is satisfied that it understands all the issues and consequences, it moves toward its decision.

Decision

This is the point of the entire process—deciding what the group will do with its resources. Which performances will continue? Which ones must begin? Which must stop? Does the group approve of its members' performances or see any need for corrective action? Is the recommendation to be accepted or rejected? What adjustments does the news require? These decisions are literally matters of life and death for programs, projects, departments and jobs. It is important that the decision-making process be rational, so the two forms of rational group decision-making will be explained in some detail in this chapter.

Commissioning

When a group has made its decision, it concludes the discussion by taking time to confirm everyone's understanding of the rationale and consequences. Commissioning answers the questions most critical to implementing the decision: Are all members able to explain the reasons for the decision? Will their explanations be consistent? Which members of the team will be most affected? In what specific ways will the group members implement the decision? Commissioning secures the group's commitment to its decisions, and groups can make such commitments even when the members disagree.

Rational Group Decision Making

Groups can make their decisions in many ways. They might be dominated by an individual or a small clique of the members; they might take votes; they might decide by indecision; they might insist on total agreement as proof of group cohesion and loyalty. (This is *not* the same as consensus decision making, which is discussed later). All these forms of group decision making have shown themselves to be fundamentally irrational. They encourage all kinds of overt and covert power play before, during and after meetings—wheeling and dealing, persuasion, selling and intimidation are common tactics. Sooner or later, many group members will stop daring to question the group's dominant power blocks—disagreement becomes too dangerous. Increasingly, "group" decisions preserve the power and resources of the dominant block. Serious thinking, innovation and creativity are stifled. Eventually the group can become so conservative that it actually chokes itself to death. It fails, while everyone pretends to be in agreement right up to the last breath.

All irrational processes have something in common—in one form or another, they all rely on threats and punishment as a method of influence. If we fail to support the dominant power block, for example, we or our department lose a lot of resources in the next round of budgeting. More common, however, are the less overt tactics of social exclusion and character assassination. When we don't "go along," for example, our comments in meetings are greeted with silence, and then the discussion continues as though we hadn't said anything. We are often interrupted. No one asks for our information or opinion. The social exclusion continues after meetings, too. We aren't invited to the informal beer bash after work; no one asks us to sign a fellow employee's birthday card; no one joins our table in the cafeteria. Along with this exclusionary behavior goes badmouthing: people describe us as stubborn, thoughtless, arrogant, rude, jealous, ego-driven, insensitive, disruptive. Sooner or later, these tags get us sorted out of the organization.

An even more subtle and common killer of group rationality is the "warm-fuzzy-smother" tactic. The group's dominant block puts on a "love" campaign that catches everyone up in feeling swell about the group. Everyone is obliged to show super concern for one another as "individual human beings," above and beyond the limited concerns of work. The required signs of loyalty are enthusiastic affirmations that *"we're great."* And of course, when the time to think comes, well . . . isn't it better to "get along" and "keep the family happy" than to insist on being right? This form of motivational hype sucks most of us in, because we really do need to feel the security and warmth of group membership and identification. But we might soon find ourselves sacrificing our own minds for the sake of group harmony. Going along becomes more important than going smart. Again, the group finds itself failing—but happy!

In contrast, rational group decision-making processes enable groups to reach resolution without unanimous agreement among the members. In these processes, the intellectual integrity of each member is expected, respected and enhanced. Underlying these processes is the assumption that each person has a unique perspective, based on his or her individual heritage and life experience. The point of group discussion is to let the variety of members' perspectives enrich everyone's perceptions of reality, options and possibilities. If group members come to meetings not expecting to agree, but seeking to understand and be understood, the group can make better use of all its minds. The pressure is off—people don't have to be persuaded to change their minds to remain members of the group. Members can listen to one another for the simple purpose of understanding exactly how the other person sees things—and for the amazement of discovering that another person can look at the same situation and see things we missed or things we don't see at all. In fact, talking and listening in this way usually causes a lot of mind-changing—i.e., learning. But the learning doesn't have to result in agreement and often does not.

In all the academic and professional studies of group processes, only two methods of group decision making have been found to perpetuate rationality: consensus and consultative decision making. These unique processes permit groups to reach resolution without unanimous agreement.

Consensus Decision Making

Consensus decision making has been misunderstood over the years as "coming to unanimous agreement," or "everyone willing to go along with the group because they feel their opinions have been respectfully considered." Properly understood, consensus decision making *doesn't* require agreement or "going along." The rule of consensus is this: if any member of the group thinks that the status quo is better than any of the options the group considers, the status quo will prevail. Said another way: if we can all agree that we can do something better than the status quo, we can decide to change in that way. The process of consensus decision making cannot be used unless the status quo is an acceptable resolution. In fact, the status quo is the *favored* resolution in consensus decision making, which is one of the reasons it has shown itself to be a very wise process in real-world applications. In the real world, the status quo is never easy or safe to change. Without a strong case for change, the status quo deserves support.

When a group makes a decision by consensus, many of the members may remain in intellectual disagreement with the decision. For example, one member may prefer the status quo to any option offered by the group. So the group's decision is to remain with the status quo. The group reaches resolution, even though every member but the one who advocated the status quo thinks at least one option is better.

In another case, the group may have many alternatives to the status quo and may choose one. The one they choose is not necessarily the one they all agree is the *best* option—it is only the one that they can all agree is better than the status quo. Group members could emerge from this meeting believing that the change they have committed to support is not the best possible change, but is only an improvement on the status quo. This is not perfect agreement, either.

Consensus decision-making is a process that can keep groups smart. However, it is usually the most time-consuming of all decision-making processes, so be sure to use it only when the decision is worth the investment of time. Consensus decision making is also the most conflictual of all decision making processes. Every member of the group has the power to veto change. All someone has to do to defeat an option offered by any other member is to demonstrate that the status quo is better. This forces members to deal with one another as equals—or it tempts the members to get into some really hardball intimidation. The members must be able to spot when their fear or frustration with disagreement is leading them to sell and persuade, rather than to simply inquire about others' perspectives and disclose their own. And members must know when the exploration is worth continuing and when it is time to stop. Group work under the rule of consensus is real intellectual work! Over time, the discipline of consensus decision making will keep a group reasonable, and its discussions will be emotionally and intellectually stimulating. But the process requires a lot of self-discipline among members! It is by no means a "warm and fuzzy" group process.

Consultative Decision Making

Consultative decision making also allows the group to reach resolution without being in agreement. In this process, one of the members is the decider. Everyone knows who this person is at the beginning of the discussion. Usually deciders start the discussion by telling us what decision they would make if they were required to do so without further consultation with the group. This allows everyone to understand the decider's starting position—the mind that the discussion intends to educate. Then the group, including the decider, will build its information base and examine its options as usual. As in consensus, everyone is obliged to understand all the other members and to insist on being understood. The group's exploration of everyone's information and opinions can benefit every member of the group, but its primary purpose is to help the decider make the best possible decision. The group should do everything it can to create a rich database for the decider. When deciders decide they are obliged to give the group another chance to question and understand the decision and its rationale (commissioning). This final discussion may remind the decider of important information and can cause the decision to change. The group's work ends when all members understand the decision and its rationale.

Note, again, that all group members must *understand* the decision; they don't have to *agree* with it. Some members may believe the decider hasn't chosen the best resolution. Nevertheless, the decider's choice is the *group's* decision—the *group's* resolution and commitment.

When the discipline of consultative decision making is maintained, it is nearly as effective as consensus decision making. It, too, can keep a group smart. But it depends more upon one member, the decider, than consensus.

Usually the decider is also the group leader—often its supervisor or manager. And this is where the process sometimes begins to lose our confidence. We may suspect that the decider isn't really willing or able to learn from the group's work. Unfortunately, these suspicions are sometimes well-grounded in experience—many supervisors do come to meetings with their minds made up. The group's discussion is then merely a polite formality—a pretended respect for the members' minds. Deciders may think that by conducting a discussion they can sell the group on a particular point of view—that the group can be manipulated into believing the idea was theirs in the first place. Most people don't fall for this more than twice. We see right through the pretense and are usually offended. It is difficult to respect people who treat us this way. And of course, all these efforts to sell agreement violate the basic assumptions of rational decision making.

But we should also remember that managers become this way in part because of the way people often act in meetings. They can't expect to learn anything valuable from us if we haven't done our homework before the meeting. If we don't keep learning, we'll have nothing to teach our managers. Our own nominal group behavior leads managers to believe that we don't really understand or care about anyone but ourselves. And when this is the case, the manager hasn't any reason to pay attention to our advice.

Managers have a larger domain of responsibility—the whole group's performance—and if we aren't willing to learn to think at their level of responsibility, we aren't any good as consultants. If we stay isolated or stagnant in our jobs, a wise manager will know that we are not really consultants, but lobbyists for our own interests and thus, more or less narrow-minded, naive and biased. Until we become informed thinkers about the whole group's performance, our managers can't afford to take our advice.

The point is that the decider and all the rest of us will have to work together to build a smart team—one that is able to use consultative decision making. We all have steep learning curves to climb, and it usually takes at least two years for all of us to become worthy consultants. While we are moving up the learning curve, we can earn one another's trust. One way to do this is always to begin the consultative process by having the deciders announce their starting position and rationale. During the discussion, everyone must listen carefully to see whether the group really does bring well-informed options into consideration. When the decision is finally made, compare it to the decider's starting position to see whether there is any evidence of learning. Did the decision change? Did it change for good reasons, or as a polite and trivial concession, or as an abdication to group intimidation? If the decision didn't change, is the original rationale now stronger, built by the group's additional information and opinions? Is it stronger because the rationale has successfully withstood probing from the group's minds? Unchanged positions can be legitimate resolutions of the group's work—if the group's information truly hasn't been ignored. Otherwise, the group has stopped working as a group—it has wasted everyone's time. Somebody, as tactfully and safely as necessary (e.g., anonymously) needs to help the decider get the message that the group is feeling misused.

As trust grows, groups will feel free to end their meetings with a brief evaluation of their decision process. One of the best methods for this is the +/- meeting evaluation. Draw a line down the middle of a white board or flip chart, and label the two columns plus and minus. Then ask the group to name quickly the things that they thought contributed positively and negatively to the group's rational decision-making process (note: no blame allowed; that's a victim tactic). When the lists have been made, ask which one or two of the negative items should be fixed in the next meeting. Circle these items, and ask the group to suggest and decide what it can do to remove or diminish these items in the next meeting.

Disagree and Commit

The last step in the basic process for Regular Meetings is *Commissioning*. This is the brief period, after the decision is made, during which the group takes account of the actions the decision will require. It is a time to align the group members' commitments.

No discussion of rational decision making is complete without some mention of the discipline to *"Disagree and Commit."* The quality of group thinking depends upon everyone's efforts to respect and preserve disagreement. But how will a group ever get to action if the members don't agree? The answer is obvious: we must often act in ways that don't fit our personal perception of the ideal. Most of the time, we must be pragmatic rather than perfect. But this is no excuse for unethical or careless conduct. As we shall see, to be effectively pragmatic, we must nourish our ideals—our visions of perfection.

Commitment is not necessarily a *feeling*—it isn't always accompanied by emotions of enthusiasm and conviction. Often, it is accompanied by anxiety and even dread (think of marriage, pregnancy, religious vows). Regardless of what people feel, however, the *behaviors* of commitment must be consistent—especially if rational group decision making is to succeed.

The first behavior of commitment is to be able to explain, accurately and completely, the rationale behind the group's decision. Sometimes this explanation may have to identify things that the group did not take into consideration. Groups aren't perfect either, and our explanation of what happens in meetings doesn't have to make them seem so.

Time may be limited in some circumstances, but it is almost always important to offer as much explanation as possible to others affected by the decision. The explanation helps others understand what is being expected and how the decision was made. This increases the group's ability to commit to the decision as well, and makes it possible for them to evaluate intelligently whether the decision is achieving its intended results. The explanation helps others stay in their Breakthrough Systems as they perform their part of the work.

A second behavior of commitment involves focusing all the resources under our control to comply with the decision. This usually involves both our own work performance—the materials, equipment, procedures and outputs we personally handle—and the performances of those we supervise and those in our Role Sets. We must make it clear to everyone with whom we work that our own behavior will align with the decision, and that we expect them to act in ways that support the decision, too. Essentially what we do is change our Performance Plan so that it reflects the group's decision, and advocate this new Performance Plan. Our commitment to the group's decision means that we will use our formal authority and informal influence to make the idea an operational reality.

Maintaining Integrity

But the behaviors of commitment do *not* include pretending to agree with the decision in one's own mind! This is one of the old definitions of "loyalty" that has caused a lot of us to look pretty stupid. People who once thought we were at least normally intelligent and understandable may have given up on us because we keep coming back from meetings acting like brainwashed cult members or whipped wimps! When we misunderstand commitment as pretended conviction or as suppression of all further discussion, we lose our reputations for intellectual integrity. We become untrustworthy because we seem to be following orders that we don't understand or care enough to question. No intelligent organization is characterized by blind obedience, and most of us know that any requirement for blind obedience is not only personally offensive, but dangerous for the future of our organization.

Contrary to the old definition of loyalty, those of us who really care about our organization will encourage disagreement not only during the group's deliberations, but also after the decision is put into action. When we come out of a meeting with our Performance Plan revised—explaining the rationale for the new decision and demonstrating to others our intention to comply—we will also let people know what options to the decision were considered and which of these, if any, we thought especially good. This not only represents the rationality of the group's decision-making process, it also keeps all the options alive. As soon as our implementation efforts disprove the wisdom of the operating commitments, or circumstances change significantly, the organization will be able to alter its path quickly. We won't have to go back and reinvent all the options. They will have been identified and explored in the first group discussions and will have continued to be refined by at least informal consideration.

When we act like this, our behavior perpetuates respect for intellectual integrity and expresses our respect for minds and learning. We create a work environment in which we are able to act in a focused and cooperative way, and in which everyone is expected to keep thinking about what we are doing. We are expected to keep listening to the feedback our actions provoke. When our goals are not being met, we are expected to question the goals and/or the way we are using resources. We are expected to revive or invent better alternatives. And we will know how to get our ideas considered quickly, because we will know which individuals and groups are responsible for the decisions that must be made. We will be in the boat where all members sit facing forward, paddling hard and talking to each other to make sure that the boat is on the right course.

When all members of the group understand clearly (and can explain) the rationale for a decision and the changes it implies for their use of resources, commissioning is over and the decision-making process is complete. If the whole process respects and encourages disagreement, the decision will be enriched by consideration of as much information and as many possible interpretations of the situation as possible. The group's resolution can be achieved in an environment of thorough, mutual understanding, but not necessarily of agreement. And the resolution can become operational reality—continuously and critically evaluated—by virtue of the members' willingness to disagree and commit.

But what if the group's decision asks us to commit to something that we believe is flatly unethical or illegal? For instance, what if the group decides to do something that misrepresents the organization's financial or scientific knowledge, violates the proprietary rights of competitors, significantly harms the environment, exposes people to unnecessary danger or violates people's civil rights? Unfortunately, such decisions are being made far too often in organizations, and they get implemented because so many of us "go along" more or less consciously.

Our choice is obvious. When we are asked to commit to things that violate our deeply held values, we can change our values, or we can stand up for them by refusing to comply. This refusal to commit may cause the group to reconsider the morality and legality of its action. Perhaps the group will then learn and grow toward the resistor's values. But the group is just as likely to react defensively and expel the resistor. The exclusion may only be informal, or it may involve demotion or termination. The pressure to comply in these cases can be enormous—to resist sometimes requires heroic courage and personal sacrifice. But after considering our personal authority and responsibility, some of us may nonetheless choose to resist, to say "I cannot, in good conscience, participate in implementing this decision. If the organization will not reconsider and insists on holding me accountable for compliance, I must resign!"

Let's Integrate Performance Plans and Work Reviews

The final point to be made about Regular Meetings is that they present opportunities to build and maintain our Performance Plans. One way to advocate a Performance Plan is to share it with the members of all the Regular Meetings we attend. We can at least do this verbally and informally while we wait for the meeting to begin or in the hallways afterward. But it is also very appropriate to write down the Plan and use it as the format in which we report our performance during Operations Reviews. Keeping the Operations Review activities of Regular Meetings and our Performance Plans in the same format simplifies our task of advocacy; it also assures lots of the necessary repetition.

We must remember to use the same Performance Plan—the one with *all* our commitments and intentions—in all the different Regular Meetings we attend. When we are in several teams, for example, it is important for the members of each team to understand all our commitments. This allows everyone to fully understand and support each other in balancing the priorities within our roles. In projects that involve several teams, it is important for the members of the other teams to understand our commitment to the joint project in relation to the other priorities that occupy our attention. It is also important to remind our regular team that we are a part of the multi-team effort as well and to explain how those commitments affect our performance in the regular group.

It helps to encourage the members of all the groups in which we participate to share their Performance Plans. This is how the group members begin to learn everyone's part of the work—how we develop our capacity to act as a fully informed consultant to the group leader. If an Operations Review using Performance Plans is not yet at the center of the Regular Meetings we attend, we should start pushing for it. In the meantime, we should at least get to know the other members' Performance Plans informally.

Of course, the leaders of all the Regular Meetings we attend should have Performance Plans, too. All the performances for which the group is responsible should be summarized in the leader's Plan. The Plan will serve as a "wiring diagram" that shows members how their group ties into the larger network of the organization. By frequently reviewing the Performance Plans of group members and leaders, everyone starts to understand who talks to whom about what, when. The information empowers everyone by making clear the information channels and the meetings where people make decisions that control the organization's resources.

Because Regular Meetings are about exercising formal authority, they deserve a lot of attention. They are our best opportunities for influencing how work gets done. Changing our behavior in meetings is probably the single most significant thing that we can do to make sure that our organizations stay focused, fast and flexible. That's the formula for organizational success, social progress and personal success at work.

Task Forces—Preparing Recommendations for Regular Meetings

Thinking—The Function of Task Forces

Another group infinitely more effective than a nominal group is the Task Force. It's a special, *temporary* group called together to think about one particular situation and to recommend what the organization should do. Once the Task Force makes its recommendation, it disbands—it lives and dies with its task.

The only purpose of a Task Force is to think. Everything about it is designed to accomplish this purpose. It should only think about three things: a decision, a problem and/or a plan.

When the Task Force analyzes a *problem*, it looks for causes and figures out how to remove them. The Task Force's recommendation describes how to diminish or correct the problem, and how much the solution will cost. When the group analyzes a *decision*, it considers several options and tries to determine which is most cost-effective for the organization. The Task Force will recommend that option. When the Task Force looks at a *plan*, it sets or confirms given goals; determines the steps to take toward those goals; establishes an efficient sequence and schedule for those steps; indicates which resources will be required at each step; and designs a system for monitoring and directing the implementation. The Task Force's recommendation is a presentation of the plan.

On many occasions, of course, the members of a Regular Meeting will do this kind of work themselves, conducting themselves as a Task Force. But members of a Regular Meeting may also decide to charter a Task Force that includes other members. That is especially appropriate when:

♦ the problems, decisions or plans are very *complex*;

♦ the group is dealing with a lot of *incomplete data*; and/or

♦ the decision is *high risk*—i.e., the consequences of making the wrong decision are very serious.

Under any of those conditions, it's a good idea to look around for the brightest and best minds in the entire organization and industry, and to involve them in this high-level intellectual work.

Choosing the Members

Under conditions of complexity, incomplete data or high risk, the Task Force should include three kinds of relevant subject-matter experts: those with access to the relevant information; those familiar with the particular type of problem, decision or plan; and those who understand technical or logistic constraints on the organization's capacity.

People with access to the relevant information might be research librarians who can help the group search the vast databases now available on nearly every subject. They might also be graduate-school students who have spent two or three years studying these databases.

Gaps in the group's database are likely to appear, however, so the Task Force will need people familiar with the issues to plug those gaps with educated guesses and well-informed opinion. People especially good at logic or complex puzzle-solving are also helpful when the group starts interpreting its database.

Finally, the group needs some experts on the organization's technical constraints and capacities. When the group gets ready to recommend some action, it must be able to estimate what the various options will cost. The group will need to know what resources the organization already has and how much will have to change if the organization adopts the recommendation. People who know the organization's processes, machines and people will be helpful at this stage of the group's work.

The Task Force may go anywhere inside or outside the organization to find the people it needs for this work. Some will be "permanent" members of the (temporary) Task Force and will serve for the entire process; others may just participate for a short time, to teach the permanent members some part of the necessary information. The permanent members need to be more than relevant experts; they must also be skilled in teaching, learning and the rational processes of decision making. The better prepared, relevant and skilled at group work these members of the Task Force are, the better their recommendations are likely to be.

The Basic Process

During the first half of its time together, an effective Task Force will spend its time building a common database. The members teach and learn until all the members understand the available information. During the second stage of its work, the Task Force identifies and compares all the possible interpretations of its database. This usually takes another 30 percent of the Task Force's total time. Finally, the Task Force decides which alternative to recommend through a consensus or consultative process.

Task Force Basic Process

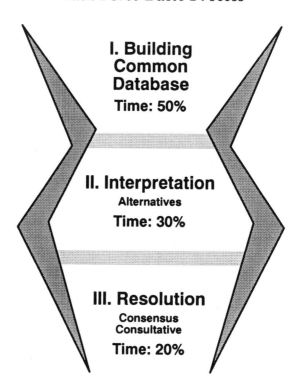

I. Building
Common
Database
Time: 50%

II. Interpretation
Alternatives
Time: 30%

III. Resolution
Consensus
Consultative
Time: 20%

As the Task Force proceeds through these three stages—database building, interpretation and resolution—disagreements among members usually arise. The first stage of learning is relatively peaceful, but the second stage *depends* on disagreement. If there is no disagreement about interpretations, there is no need for the group. The resolution stage is often very difficult as well, because some well-informed and experienced members will believe the group's resolution is not exactly what it should be. The level of conflict at these stages is a pretty reliable measure of the quality of the group's work. If a Task Force finds resolution in the middle of complex, uncertain and high-risk situations without experiencing any differences of opinion, one should wonder whether the right people were included, and whether they took their assignment seriously.

Reaching resolution is not the end of the Task Force's work, however. Once the group has formulated its recommendation, the members of the Task Force should break out as individuals or in pairs and educate all the key stakeholders in the organization— those who will be most affected by the recommendation. This task is *not* a sales job. The members of the Task Force are not obliged to lobby for the recommendation. As participants in the decision-making process, they were obliged to ensure that the process was reasonable and led to a rational recommendation. But they are not required to be sure the recommendation is *accepted*.

An organization may have many good reasons for rejecting a good recommendation; and the reasons usually relate to organizational resource issues. For example, the recommended action may not compete favorably with other opportunities the organization has for using the same resources. The organization may decide, after it understands the situation and proposed resolution, that this is the wrong time to take the recommended action—other efforts and investments may need to mature first. The Task Force is not responsible for considering these variables—that is the work of people who actually control the resources—the members of the organization's Regular Meetings.

A Task Force's education effort is not lobbying. It just ensures that each key stakeholder has a chance to understand the recommendation and rationale in a safe and unofficial setting. During these informal discussions, the Task Force members provide a full review of their group's proceedings. They answer questions about how the database was formed, which alternatives were considered, and how the group arrived at its resolution. The Task Force members may even explain their personal disagreements with the recommendation, as long as they also describe how the group dealt with these disagreements and arrived at its different conclusion. For Task Force members, commitment means the behavior of faithfully explaining the group's rationale for its resolution; it does not mean pretending to agree or ignoring reservations. The education task is finished when key stakeholders understand the recommendation; they don't have to agree with it, either.

While the education process is taking place, the Task Force members should get together to share what is happening in the discussions with key stakeholders. If, in these discussions, members learn that the Task Force has failed to consider important information or alternatives, the group has not done its job sufficiently well. The Task Force needs to think through its recommendation again.

It is quite possible during this education period that many key stakeholders will disagree with the recommendation. As long as their disagreements are based on organizational resource issues— not on discoveries that the Task Force ignored important information or alternatives, or miscalculated the consequences of its recommendation—the Task Force should persist with its recommendation. The group has not failed if its recommendation is rejected because of resource problems. It fulfills its responsibility when it presents the Regular Meeting authorities with a recommendation backed by a complete and accurate analysis that addresses the assigned situation.

To be invited to serve on a Task Force is usually a compliment to one's expertise and skills in group work. But such an invitation is not merely an honor, it is also an obligation. The disciplines of Task Force membership are: serious preparation for each session; readiness for teaching and learning; stamina and patience; and insistence on intellectual integrity. Task Forces are meetings in which the group does *work*. From these groups, an organization gets its brilliant options—solutions for its problems, new strategies and reliable plans for a better future. Task Force meetings influence the future of our organizations. They are very serious work.

Summary: Let's Really Meet

As the cliché goes, no one is an island. We must manage ourselves, but we must also coordinate with others, and thus we participate in managing them. Others, in turn, participate in managing us. Some of this happens informally through the operation of

Role Sets, but much of it happens very deliberately and officially, through our participation in Regular Meetings and Task Forces.

If we leave behind the self-defeating habits of nominal groups, we can make meetings into places where people work cooperatively. We can go to meetings expecting to understand and be understood; we can expect and respect disagreement during and after meetings; we can accept that sometimes, for pragmatic reasons, we will have to commit to actions that are less than perfect, while the group learns better ways to do its work. In these ways, we will help sustain rational cooperation and intellectual integrity.

The world's demand for quality products and services is never-ending, and each person's power to meet the demand multiplies exponentially through cooperative thinking and action. As thinking people, sharing information, authority and commitments, each of us can help create organizations that are both healthy and very productive.

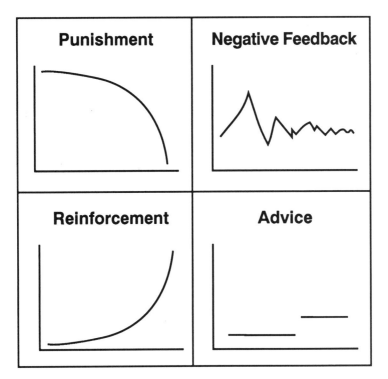

| Punishment | Negative Feedback |
| Reinforcement | Advice |

Accelerating Learning and Change

Using Our Brains for
a Change

* * * *

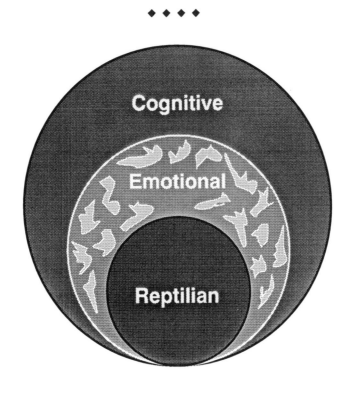

Overview

Because our organizations are in a state of continuous change, we must continuously learn. Learning is the personal form of change—i.e., we change our own habits or skills. This chapter explains how the brain functions in learning and explores ways to assist and accelerate that process.

The workplace is rich with opportunities to learn. When we experience distress, however, our brains try to help by moving immediately to their best-known responses—our habits. To do this, our brains actually "turn off" or "downshift" the cognitive functions that allow us to learn.

Four kinds of performance feedback get our attention: *advice, encouragement, negative feedback* and *punishment*. These will be discussed in detail in Chapter 10. All four types of feedback imply change and create some distress. But two of them—punishment and negative feedback—are especially likely to cause people's brains to downshift. Unfortunately, workplaces are full of such messages, and they harm everyone's ability to learn and change.

There are some things that we can do to help ourselves avoid downshifting in specific situations. We can practice the "Three A's of Emotional Control." The first is to Acknowledge the emotions—simply to name them and notice their intensity. The next step is to Accept the emotions—understanding that they are the symptoms of habits that move into action to help us deal with stressful situations. Often, we may need to remove ourselves from such situations temporarily, to relax and reflect on how we learned our habits and how they serve us. After this Acceptance, we can move toward Action. We can either affirm that the habit is perfectly appropriate, or choose to learn a new one. When we decide to learn, we look for a new pattern of behavior, try it, and if we like it, practice it until it becomes a new habit. The process described by the "Three A's" is a way of getting all the tissues of our brains working together toward learning.

Key Concepts

 ♦ The human brain can be roughly divided into three parts: *reptilian, emotional* and *cognitive*. To learn, all three parts must be operating.

- In conditions of distress, the brain downshifts—turns off its cognitive and sometimes its emotional parts—and makes learning impossible.
- Some performance-feedback messages, especially punishment and negative feedback, usually create distress and make learning difficult.
- We can learn to avoid downshifting in specific situations by using the "Three A's of Emotional Control"—Acknowledgment, Acceptance and Action.

Possible Activities

- Discuss the experience and symptoms of downshift at work.
- Identify some specific cases in which performance feedback caused downshift.
- Practice (alone) the "Three A's of Emotional Control" to learn a new habit.

Three-Part Brain—A Theory about How We Learn

Learning and Changing

Earlier chapters frequently mention the need to learn constantly. The nature of work is changing—becoming faster, more complex and more precise. The pace of change isn't likely to slow down anytime during our careers. Where circumstances change quickly and frequently, learning is an essential survival skill. We must keep learning so that our organizations can keep delivering quality products and services to customers. This chapter and the next explain some things that we can do to make the process of learning and changing easier for ourselves and each another.

Much has been discovered in recent decades about the learning process. Old theories are falling away as we test them through research. Some of us may think, for example, that "you can't teach an old dog new tricks"—that as we get older, our ability to learn new habits and skills diminishes. In fact, human beings can continue learning and changing until the day they die. As long as the brain is not diseased or damaged, its capacity for learning only gets better with age.

Researchers are also noticing that extraordinary intelligence isn't essential for achieving economic success or creating socially useful products and services. People with normal intelligence and lots of persistence are more likely to succeed in those ways.

Some research also indicates that economic status has little to do with one's *ability* to learn, though it does affect the *content* that one is likely to learn. Another finding is that when people are placed in radically changed environments, most demonstrate an ability to make radical changes in behavior, usually by accelerating their learning.

Yet most of us experience our own and others' resistance to learning every day. We might experience this resistance as irritation, for example, when we call a doctor and reach a seemingly endless labyrinth of recorded messages and voice-mail boxes; or when we drive up to a gas station and discover that we're expected to run the pump and cash register with our own credit cards; or when we attend a Regular Meeting at work and are confronted with statistical process-control charts. These situations can leave us feeling so puzzled and helpless that we don't even know where to start thinking about them.

And sometimes we find it almost impossible to think in the face of others' behavior. We think they're "jerking our chains" with some sort of insult or threat, and we find ourselves snapping and snarling right back. And then there are times when we know perfectly well what changes we should make, but we feel intimidated by our Role Sets to remain as we are. If we are to take advantage of our own abilities to learn, we need to know enough about the learning process to be able to handle these kinds of situations. Some theoretical information about how we learn and change behavior can be very useful.

Our Reptilian, Emotional and Cognitive Brains

Learning is the means to behavioral change, and behavior is determined by brain functions. This section is not meant to be a physiology textbook, but it will explain some basics about how brain physiology affects learning and resistance to learning. The brain is actually designed to do both—change and resist change—because each of those acts is essential to survival under different circumstances.

The human brain can be described as having three distinct parts: *the reptilian brain, the emotional brain* and *the cognitive brain.*

The Brain: Learning and Change

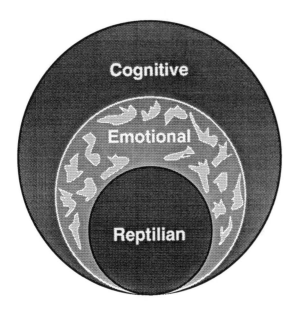

The reptilian brain controls the autonomic functions of our bodies: breathing, heartbeat, body temperature, hunger, sex drive. In high-tech terms, it is *hard-wired.* We get our reptilian brain through heredity, and there isn't much we can do to change it. This part of our brain is buried in the center of our skulls. It has maximum protection from head injury, because it controls the most vital organs of survival. It operates continuously with a precision that can be measured in fractions of a second. Many living creatures, such as snakes and lizards, have only this much of a brain. They live their lives on automatic pilot—by instinct. A fly goes by and a reptile's tongue snaps out; it's not a decision, it's an irresistible compulsion.

When we are reduced to operating from only this part of our brains, our lives aren't much different from those of reptiles.

Another set of tissues surrounds the core reptilian brain and controls body chemistry essential to action and bodily adaptation. When this part of the brain operates, it causes us to experience what we call emotions. In contrast to the hard-wired reptilian brain, the emotional brain is like computer software; it operates on changeable programs. The emotional brain puts chemicals into our bloodstream and signals into our nervous system in response to cues (stimuli) in our body and in the external environment. Even at fetal stages of development, humans learn to identify environmental cues and associate them with experiences of pain and pleasure. As infants, for example, loud voices and crashing sounds will be recognized as warnings of imminent violence. Other cues such as humming, rocking and the smell of mother's skin may signal the pleasures of nourishment. This is the most basic type of learning.

Soon, we also learn behaviors that help us deal with experiences of pain and pleasure. We learn to curl up and turn away when loud sounds occur; we may learn that crying can cause the pleasures of nourishment to begin. For us to perform these actions, the organs of the emotional brain must coordinate chemical messages dropped into our bloodstreams and electrical charges sent through our nervous systems. Every time these actions lead to pleasure and help us avoid pain, we strengthen the neural network in the emotional brain that links our active responses to the recognized cues. The operation of these well-worn neural networks is what we experience and describe as "natural," "spontaneous," "automatic" responses. They are, in fact, well-memorized learned responses—habits.

This type of learning continues throughout our lives, but it is important to understand that it begins very early. Long before we are able to use language to think and communicate, we interact emotionally with our environment—we learn when to duck, when to cry, when to smile, when to make soft gurgling sounds. And we form basic assumptions about our place in the environment—we may begin to see ourselves as victims or as empowered players. By the time we have survived long enough to speak, we will have learned some very important survival habits and will be operating from some well-entrenched assumptions. Because we develop these habits without the assistance of language, most of us experience them as completely automatic—beyond our intellectual understanding or control. But research reveals that even these early habits, as well as all the later ones, can be reprogrammed through learning.

Although the reptilian brain operates in very short time frames, the emotional brain is capable of sustaining its "programs" for up to 30 minutes. It has sophisticated wait-and-see, look-before-leaping, try-this-then-that kinds of patterns that can keep our bodies ready to respond to external cues for as long as a half hour. But the habitual behavior controlled by the emotional brain rarely operates on a planning horizon of more than 30 minutes. Unless the programs are stimulated by a repetition of the associated cues, they "phase out." By the time we become adults, however, we have usually developed enough of these habits that we can get through at least 80 percent of each day without ever operating beyond the capacities of our reptilian and emotional brains.

Many other living creatures have these two-part brains. Perhaps the best illustration is a dog. Notice how authentic and spontaneous dogs are in expressing their emotions. We don't have to be around them for long before their emotional states become perfectly transparent—from panting happiness to snarling hatred. Especially in their early years, dogs are remarkably trainable. Some people suggest that humans should live with similar spontaneity and authenticity, and that's all right for those who don't aspire to anything more than a dog's life.

The third portion of the brain is cognitive. This part comprises 75 percent of a human's brain mass, and it is what separates humans most from other animals. Anthropologists who study the development of human skeletons have noticed that the skull has changed significantly through the millennia. It has changed to make more room for this third, outer layer of brain tissue. Evidence suggests that in the scheme of evolution, this third layer of brain provides special advantages for human survival.

The special function of this third layer of brain tissue is called *cognition*—abstract thinking, the ability to create models of reality. The most important of these modeling methods is language—words are how we think and communicate about external and internal phenomena. Time, cause-and-effect, relationships, math, logic, music and law are other such modeling methods. On the basis of such models, we are able to make predictions. We can get out of the emotional brain's 30-minute window and consider light years and infinity. Cognitive models are the means by which we have promoted human existence through religion, law, art and technology. Furthermore, cognitive tissues must be involved when we want to reprogram our habits and develop new skills.

How the Parts of the Brain Interact To Learn

A simple but fundamentally correct way of understanding how our brains function in learning is to imagine the process as a dialogue between the emotional and cognitive brains. The emotional brain, in pursuit of happiness, goes along from opportunity to opportunity, triggering first one habitual response and then another. Each success causes the emotional brain to try the same response again, so that its neural paths get worn into deep, fast tracks. We start trying to fix every problem with the same hammer, so to speak, and of course, much of the time we just make a mess—until the cognitive brain interrupts the pattern of behavior with a question:

Cognitive: "Are you sure that's the same kind of problem you once fixed with a hammer? Notice that your target is not actually a nail—it's a bolt."

Emotional: "Oh yeah. I know what a bolt is. Sure enough, it's a bolt."

Cognitive: "Do you want the bolt to hold those beams together?"

Emotional: "Yeah, that's why I'm going to hit it with this hammer."

Cognitive: "Is that working?"

Emotional: "Not very well. Not like when I hit a nail."

Cognitive: "Have you ever made a bolt work?"

Emotional: "No, not actually."

Cognitive: "Ever seen anyone else make one work?"

Emotional: "Yeah . . . once."

Cognitive: "Did she use a hammer?"

Emotional: "No, she had some other funny-looking thing, it didn't look nearly as good as my hammer, though."

Cognitive: "But it made the bolt work?"

Emotional: "Yeah, I believe so."

Cognitive: "How did it work—how did it make the beams hold together?"

Notice how slowly this dialogue is going. The poor old emotional brain just wants to act! If the cognitive brain doesn't keep reminding it of its opportunity—getting the beams bolted together—the emotional brain will lose interest, wander off, and find some other nail—or bolt, or screw, or rivet, or pipe, or pencil, or arrow—to hit. But if the cognitive brain can hold the emotional brain's attention long enough, it will eventually discover an alternative to the hammer and provide encouragement while the emotional brain practices the new response more appropriate to bolts. And of course, we can't forget that the reptilian brain is in the background steadily keeping the pumps running while these other two parts of the brain are busy being amazed.

Another fictional illustration: In the beginning, no one hunted lions. Hunters tried to avoid lions at all costs while hunting other game. They had learned from terrible experiences that movement in the grass meant scream and run like crazy. Don't even pause to make sure it's a lion, because if it is, you'll be dead! Scream-and-run, in this case, needed to happen without thinking—it needed to be a habit.

Another useful habit went like this: If, while hunting in a group, one of the other hunters begins screaming and running, everyone else starts running and screaming, too. Get everyone running so that if we don't all succeed in outrunning the lion, at least only one of us is taken. This seemed best for the survival of the hunting party.

Perhaps one day when a hunter heard the warning screams of other hunters, he looked up and saw an approaching lion. Instead of running, the hunter froze in panic; he went absolutely as still as a statue. And a funny thing happened—the lion ran right past and chased someone else.

Later, at the evening campfire, the frightened hunter probably told the story like this: "I couldn't move. The lion was so close; I knew it had me! I went still like the dead meat I knew I was. But then, the lion looked away and sprang after one of the others who was running."

During the storytelling session, the hunters' cognitive brains went to work, remembering and making comparisons. The hunters probably recognized that this story didn't fit the model of what to do when a lion is in the grass. As the hunters collected more of these stories, about lions running right past easy targets, someone finally altered the model, saying, "Maybe lions have trouble seeing things that don't move. Maybe instead of running, we ought to stand very still." (As a matter of fact, this is true. Lions prefer moving targets.) With some practice—which the early hunters called "lion dancing"—a new habit moved into their bag of tricks: i.e., in the presence of a lion, stand very still—look to see whether it intends to attack.

As a result of this behavior, even more new data could be collected through storytelling sessions. Hunters eventually figured out that most of the lions they saw were sound asleep or half-asleep and very unlikely to attack. Screaming and running only woke them up and excited them to attack.

Once again, the hunters' cognitive tissues went to work and invented another new option. Since the lion is sleeping, why not attack it? The hunters worked out this option with more lion-dancing. Eventually they turned the tables; instead of being the prey, the hunters became the predators.

This bit of fiction illustrates how the emotional and cognitive parts of the brain interact to learn. First the old habit must be broken—by accident (as in our story), or by deliberate interruption. Then the cognitive brain must analyze the situation and work out optional responses (storytelling). Finally the options must be practiced and tested until they become a new habit (lion-dancing). The process of learning involves the whole human brain: all three parts. The process depends, of course, upon the maintenance functions of the reptilian brain. It also requires us to evaluate cues and be ready to take action—the habit-management functions of the emotional brain. Finally, the process requires us to consider alternatives and options, which the cognitive brain's modeling capacities make possible. Without the whole brain in operation, learning cannot take place.

A Theory about Why We Don't Learn— Downshifting Our Brains

Although the whole brain is required for learning, the whole brain doesn't function most of the time. The reptilian and emotional brains are sufficient for most of our survival. We have been able to get by with a small collection of clever and well-rehearsed habits. Because we rarely need anything more, we don't have much motive for learning. After watching ourselves and others for a while, it's easy to arrive at the conclusion that adults lose the capacity to learn. This isn't true—it's not that we lose the capacity, it's just that learning hasn't seemed necessary. Perhaps our jobs weren't too difficult, and they seemed to have a long future in which the only changes would be further simplifications. One explanation for why learning doesn't occur is that in many situations, we just don't need to do it.

Downshifting—How Our Brains Sometimes Protect Us from Learning

But there is another explanation for why learning doesn't occur, which is more important to understand these days. When we are confronted with emergencies, we don't feel that we can afford the time to learn. Part of our response to stressful situations occurs in the brain: the process called "downshifting."

In situations that we interpret as stressful, our brain does us a favor—it refuses to learn. It's as if our brain says, "Storm! Batten down the hatches and put on the life jackets! It's time for fast, efficient response: pull out the ready-made habits!" And the first part of the brain that gets sealed off is the cognitive brain. The cognitive tissues are actually deactivated by the reptilian and emotional brains. Those two parts send one clear message to the cognitive tissues: "Shut up! This is no time for idle chatter; we have to act!" Then they slam the physiological doors that allow further communication.

When a downshift occurs, we experience intense emotion. When confronted by a hostile person, for example, mild anxieties become well-focused fear, and we tremble with readiness to act. In our excitement, we try all our tricks: "My smile-off isn't working, can I create a distraction? How does apology and begging for forgiveness work? I don't think I can out-run him; I'd better hit him with a hammer!" Our condition of emotional excitement makes it impossible for us to think—it's no time to try to read the diagrams of a karate handbook, let alone figure out the situation's legal implications. In these moments, we turn to the behaviors that have worked for us in the past and hope that they will work again. We have all our ready-made skills to apply, but in these moments we are not intelligent in the way we must be to learn new skills.

Downshift in the brain can go even further. The emergency can be so severe that the reptilian brain says to the emotional brain, "Sorry, no time for your hysterics." Then it slams the door on the emotional brain, too. At this stage, we are in sheer panic.

One of the circumstances in which many people experience panic is an automobile accident. When the trauma has passed, we are amazed by what we remember (long-term memory involves the reptilian brain). The whole experience replays in our minds as if in slow motion. Sometimes we remember terrified expressions on the faces of people in the other car just before we collided. We might remember hearing the crunch of metal, the flashes of flying glass, the momentum of the car spinning, the feel of our own flesh and bones being damaged. And we seem to have been removed somehow from the whole experience, as passionless observers of even our own suffering.

Sometimes, after panic has passed, we are amazed by what we were able to do. We may realize a pit bull dog is snarling and slamming itself against the other side of a seven-foot fence that we were somehow able to jump over! Or we realize that we just lifted the rear end of an automobile with one hand and pulled a child out from under the tire with the other. Or we find out that we've just run two miles on a broken leg, after escaping a forest fire. Of course, some people are destroyed when they act in panic: by swimming into a flash flood to save a friend, jumping from the upper stories of a burning building, or attacking a gang of armed muggers. When the reptilian brain takes over in panic, people often find themselves doing things that they've never done before—things they would never do "in their right minds." Primitive programs of behavior take over—instinctual flight-or-fight reactions. These, too, are favors our brain does for us—helping us try one more thing when we have no relevant habits for the situation and reason would point out that "all is lost."

We must respect how beautifully our brains defend and promote our well-being. Downshifting is not wrong; it is a survival strategy. And downshifting isn't unusual—most of us experience it every day. But downshifting *does* stop our learning. The first step in developing or teaching any new skill involves recognizing when our brains are downshifted.

Symptoms of Downshift

Visual Symptoms	Audible Symptoms
Complexion changes—goes pale or blushes	Voice
	Gets louder or softer
Eyes change—pupils contract or expand	Goes higher in pitch
Tears form	Breathing changes
Eye contact changes—aversion or staring	Speech
Jaw clenches	Starts or stops
Lips purse	Becomes faster or slower
Head shakes from side to side	Becomes insulting or threatening
Movements become stiff or jerky	Is delivered through clenched teeth
Position changes	Stutters
Moves closer	Understanding
Moves away	Person needs things to be repeated
Body seems to freeze/gets very still	Person can't seem to hear as well
Body trembles	
Body twitches	Person can't seem to understand
Breathing changes—slows or speeds up and deepens	

The Symptoms of Downshifting

The symptoms of downshifting are a little different for every-one, but they are not at all hidden or mysterious. It is easiest to learn about these symptoms by watching other people downshift. (When we are downshifted ourselves, our ability to think about this analyti-cally is limited.) We're good at noticing other people's downshift-ing symptoms, because when others downshift, they become poten-tially dangerous—excited and more-or-less out of control. To de-fend ourselves, most of us become very good at reading the signs of others' downshifts. In fact, these signs are often cues to which we respond by starting our own downshifts. The process is contagious!

Most of what we notice is a drastic change in a person's normal appearance and behavior. Any small group can make a list of at least 20 symptoms of downshift in about 3 minutes.

Once we become aware of these changes as cues that someone is downshifting, we're ready to turn our attention to ourselves. We can list what we think we do in both mild and extreme cases of downshift. Then we can find a friend and ask for feedback—what they remember about the symptoms of our downshift. Knowing this about ourselves can help us recognize when we are downshifting. Of course, the other reliable sign is that we are having more intense emotions.

Keeping Our Brains in High Gear—the Three A's for Changing Our Habits

It is possible to interrupt a downshift and turn our whole brain back on. But remember that this may not always be such a good idea. Sometimes we need the speed of our habits in order to survive or take advantage of the moment. Mastery of any skill means to respond appropriately by habit—without having to think about it. A jazz pianist can't start thinking about finger movements in the middle of performance, or the musicianship will be destroyed. The pianist must "stay with it"—remain emotionally and habitually attuned. The very point of much of our learning is to transfer skills to the control of our emotional brains, so that we can make precisely correct responses very quickly. We don't always want or need to interrupt our habitual performance. In some cases, doing so would not be intelligent.

But there are times when we're hitting a bolt with a hammer. For instance, some of us downshift every time a member of the opposite sex comes into view—and some of our habitual responses are very inappropriate at work. Some of us feel a flare of resentment and disgust at the sight of some particular workmate with whom we've had a long-standing grudge, and we just can't resist jabbing that person with another insult and getting into another of those rude shouting matches. We've damaged one another's careers this way and know it, but we just can't seem to stop it.

Some of us downshift at the sight of any authority figure, and this makes it difficult for us to get our ideas and work coordinated through the organization's network of authority. Some of us downshift as soon as two or more people look at us simultaneously, and this makes it difficult to participate in the Regular Meetings that are so important to our managing our work. In these cases, we're not making appropriate responses, given what we're trying to accomplish, and new or more refined habits are needed. When this is the case, we can use the Three A's of emotional control: Acknowledge, Accept, Act.

Three A's of Emotional Control

 **cknowledge**

Name the emotion.

How intense is the emotion?

 **ccept**

Why do I feel the way I do?

What are the cues?

When did I first learn to make this response?

 **ct**

What do I want to do?

Do I want to express my true feelings?

Acknowledge—Naming Our Emotions

As soon as we feel strong emotions coming on, we *acknowledge* the feeling. For instance, we might say to ourselves, "I'm really disappointed." Then on second thought, we might correct ourselves: "No, I'm not disappointed; I'm angry." As soon as we have named the emotion appropriately, we label its intensity. We might say to ourselves, "This anger is not too strong—it's more like irritation than rage."

We sometimes have a bad habit of misnaming our intellectual interpretations as emotions. The statements "I feel rejected," or "I feel criticized by you," for example, are actually interpretations of someone else's behavior—i.e., "that person is rejecting or criticizing me." That's a belief, not an emotion, and it may not be what the other person intends to convey at all. The actual *emotion* might be, "I feel lonely," or "I feel sad," or "I feel frightened and defensive." It takes practice to distinguish between actual emotions and interpretations of others' behavior, but it's an important skill. It enables us to avoid blaming others and behaving as victims by trying to make others somehow "responsible" for our own interpretations of and internal reactions to stimuli.

It is important to literally *talk* to ourselves. Remember that language is a function of the brain's cognitive tissues. This act of labeling feelings is a simple cognitive act. It's an immediate invitation for the cognitive brain to stay active and begin a dialogue with the emotional brain.

Accept—Understanding Our Habits

We can *accept* that the feeling we are having and the habitual response we are currently making sometimes works; it worked in the past, or it wouldn't have become a habit. The word "accept" has a positive connotation, and it is important to approach our own emotional responses positively. Our habits—even the most self-destructive ones—are always benign at some level: they intend to serve our welfare and have actually done so in the past.

To accept our emotions, we need to stop and look for the environmental cue to which we have learned to make this habitual response. What is it, specifically, that we are reacting to angrily? We might have a conversation with ourselves that goes something like this: "Della's late for the meeting again. That's the cue. But wait,

Frank came late, too, and Wanda came even later than Della. I didn't feel angry then. So what is it about Della that bugs me?" Then we look more closely at the situation; some special combination of cues is working in our brain. Notice how analytical we're getting; our cognitive brain is really getting involved.

Sometimes we won't be able to understand immediately the relationship between cue and response. Just to acknowledge and begin acceptance will usually interrupt the downshift and allow us to put the habit aside for the moment. But to change the habit in our relationship to "Della," we will need to reflect further.

The Emotions and Functions chart on page 216 identifies some relationships between cues and responses. In the left-hand column are the names of some basic emotions. In the next column are brief descriptions of action-readiness responses that each emotion causes in people's bodies. The third column mentions the function of each emotion—its general purpose. In the final column is the result the emotion helps us accomplish. Anger, for example, gets us ready to fight. Its function is to restore control in a situation. Expressing anger through action is a way to remove an obstacle to control.

In the earlier example, if we name the emotion correctly as anger, we're interpreting Della as an obstacle to our control. This suggests that some things should be explored: What are we trying to control? How is Della threatening our control? How are my current responses to Della working? Are we regaining the control that we want?

Sometimes we won't see the relationship of cue and response until we reflect on our earliest uses of the habit. In the case of Della, we might continue the dialogue with ourselves as follows: "Who does Della remind me of? She's short and chubby, walks with her head thrown back a little so that she seems to waddle, is always smiling and making funny . . . Oh! It's my aunt Annie! But I don't remember going to any meetings with Annie . . . Oh no, there it is! Unbelievable. I'm reliving dinnertime when I was about six or seven years old. My father's law was that everybody had to be at the dinner table at 6 p.m. And when Fred and Annie first came over from Ireland and lived at our house for a while, everyone but Annie made it to dinner on time. And when she was late, Dad would get mad! We were all forced to wait, and so I got mad too. We'd all give Annie a bath of cold silence through the first minutes of dinner—just like

Emotions and Functions

Emotion	Action Tendency	Function	End State
Desire	Approach	Producing situation permitting consumption	Access
Fear	Avoidance	Protection	Own inaccessibility
Enjoyment, confidence	Being-with	Permitting consumption	Contact, interaction
Interest	Attending (opening)	Orientation	Identification
Disgust	Rejecting (closing)	Protection	Removal of object
Indifference	Nonattending	Selection	No information or contact
Anger	Contention	Regaining control	Removal of obstruction
Shock, surprise	Interrupting	Reorientation	Reorientation
Arrogance	Dominating	Generalized control	Retained control
Humility, resignation	Submitting	Secondary control	Deflected pressure
Sorrow	Deactivation	(Recuperation?)	————
Effort	Bound activation	Aim achievement	Action tendency's end state
Excitement	Excitement	Readiness	————
Joy	Free activation	Generalized readiness	————
Contentment	Inactivity	Recuperation	————
Anxiety	Inhibition	Caution	Absence of response
(Laughter, weeping)	Surrender	Activation decrease or social cohesion?	Activation decrease?

Frijda, Nico H. *The Emotions: Studies in Emotion & Social Interaction.* Cambridge: Cambridge University Press, 1986. Reprinted with permission.

I'm doing in the meeting with Della! This is ridiculous—but I can feel that it's true! This is the habit with which I'm responding to Della."

This sort of understanding often frees us from the habitual response because we realize that it worked in the earlier situation when we first learned to act this way, but it is not appropriate in our current situation. A different response is possible, and it might be more effective in achieving the intent of the initial angry response: to regain some kind of control in a situation in which one feels powerless. "I'm trying to control the environment of the meeting. There's work that we need to do, and we need to do it together. We can't do it well until everyone is there. Anything we try to do has to be done again when the late people finally get there. Tardiness keeps the meeting out of control."

Act—Developing New Habits

Acknowledgment and acceptance of our emotional responses are usually private activities, although consultation with a trustworthy friend or counselor can sometimes be helpful. But as we move to the third A, which stands for *action*, we begin the process of expressing the emotion, of "going public." Keep in mind that habits are expressions of emotional responses. A habit is only one way that our emotions prepare us to act—other actions are possible. We don't ever want to get rid of our emotions, but we may want to change the habitual action for which they so quickly prepare us. We can choose to form a new habit—to find a new public expression of our emotions.

When we have acknowledged and accepted the feelings that we are having, we can deal with the question of what action to take. We begin by exploring alternatives. Have we ever *acted* differently in response to the same cue? What happened? Have we ever seen anyone else respond differently to the same cue? What happened to that person? Can we imagine other alternative responses? Are we willing to try them? Can we find a safe place to practice these responses and find out how they work for us?

In the case of Della, the exploration might go like this: "My cold, silent treatment of Della isn't causing her to come on time; she probably doesn't even know what is irritating me. I'm responding differently to the others who come late, but frankly, none of those responses is causing people to come on time, either. I think my concern for promptness in this case is reasonable—asking people to come on time is not just a symbol of authority as it was at my father's dinner table. I think I'll try going to each of the people who come late and clarify my expectations for promptness."

Now, the anger can find expression in a new behavior—talking to people about coming to the meeting on time. Expressing anger does not mean that we will storm into their work areas and rant and rave. Ranting and raving, like cold silences, are other habitual expressions of anger. They rarely succeed in removing the obstacles to human cooperation at work. The best expression of anger at work is usually the behavior of problem solving—e.g., talking about promptness at meetings. As a general rule, it is best to focus discussion on the *problem*, not our *feelings* about the problem. In fact, it's usually a good idea to wait until we have successfully set aside the other expressions of our emotions before we begin dealing with the problem. Showing a lot of emotion will only invite others to start downshifting. We might wind up sounding like hissing lizards; not like people finding a better way to cooperate.

When we find a new response that works for us, we repeat it until it comes easily in response to a cue. By doing this, we start forming a new behavioral habit. We also make it possible to operate on lower doses of the chemicals we experience as emotions. In some cases, such as anger, these chemicals can build up in the bloodstream and get deposited in body tissues as a poison. New habits of problem-solving can make our emotions safe, both for ourselves and for the others with whom we work.

With practice, acknowledgment can become nearly instantaneous. Acknowledgment alone is often sufficient to interrupt habitual responses and make room for something else to happen. Acceptance often takes a little longer, especially if the habit is deeply embedded from lifelong repetition. Fortunately, a complete analysis of the past is not necessary before action toward change can begin. The more complete the analysis, however—and thus, the more complete the acceptance—the more energy we will find available for new action.

The three A's are themselves new habits that we may need to practice for some time before they feel natural. But the personal experience of the process will greatly enrich our understanding of how learning happens and how downshifting and old habits operate to frustrate learning.

Summary: Let's Support Each Other's Learning

Our brief exploration of the brain and learning in this chapter leads to the following conclusions: Under stress, our brains downshift to take care of us by relying on well-practiced behaviors called habits. We can actually experience this happening when we feel emotions—the chemistry and electrical systems of our body get ready to act.

Living life on the basis of habits is effective and efficient to the extent that we aren't confronted with a lot of new situations. If our situations start changing a lot, then our habits will stop being effective. Our failures can lead to even more stress and cause us to enter a downward spiral—more of the same inappropriate responses, more failure, more stress.

When we need to learn new habits, we must stop the downshift—and invite the cognitive tissues of our brains back into action. The three A's—Acknowledge, Accept, Act—are a way to stop our downshifts and learn new responses. They enable us to deal with stress so that learning becomes possible.

Other strategies discussed in earlier chapters also aim at reducing the stress we experience in working together. Creating Breakthrough Systems for the tasks we perform puts us in reliable self-control. Using Performance Plans is a way to keep our Role Sets working as support groups rather than as stress hazards. Ensuring that meetings are places where we are not punished for disagreeing, where understanding and intellectual integrity are the goals also diminishes stress.

Diminishing stress for ourselves and for others is not merely a way to make the workplace nicer. Keeping stress under control makes it possible for everyone to learn. Our situation at work is changing. We have to develop new responses, new habits. We have to learn to succeed together at work.

Giving Encouragement and Advice— Coaching for Change

◆◆◆◆

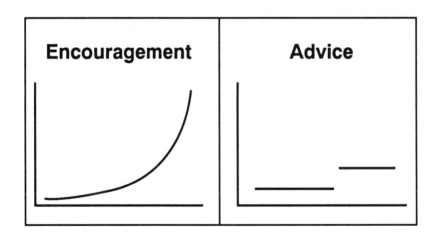

Overview

Our final chapter discusses some very specific things that can be done to make the workplace a better learning environment—ways that we can give ourselves and each other encouragement and advice.

Coaching is another way of describing encouragement and advice. It is a skill that most people can learn, and it can have a dramatic effect on the mood and performance of individuals and teams. When we follow the six guidelines for giving encouragement detailed in this chapter, we become conscious of our own strengths and start using them more. When we follow the additional six guidelines for giving advice, we transfer energy from undesirable behavior to desirable behavior. We help one another improve by working better, not harder. Effective encouragement and advice help individuals and teams improve and keep informed about this continual improvement. Respect for ourselves and our teammates grows. The team mood usually becomes one of reasonable confidence and mutual support.

It is especially appropriate to end this book with a consideration of the rules for effective coaching. The principles embodied in these coaching rules fuel the power of Role Sets, Breakthrough Systems, Performance Plans and meetings. It is important to reflect on these principles and to understand how all the concepts discussed in this book are consistent with the fundamental rules of coaching. As we deliberately increase our use of these practices, our organizations can become open systems, moving into the future with greater ability to solve problems, recognize and take advantage of opportunities and enrich society with products and services. These principles are the vehicles that will keep our organizations moving toward new breakthroughs in performance that contribute to the quality of our lives.

Key Concepts

◆ We can increase the frequency of desirable behavior through encouragement.

◆ Encouragement is not an attitude; it is a specific message that must be delivered according to six rules if it is to be effective.

- We can transfer energies from undesirable behavior to desirable behavior by giving advice.
- Advice also must be delivered according to six rules if it is to be effective.

Possible Activities

- Discuss how Breakthrough Systems enrich our work via encouragement and advice.
- Commit to offering more encouragement.

Getting Attention—Threats and Opportunities

This chapter continues the exploration of what we can do to promote learning at work. In this book, the operational definition of *learning* is behavioral change—changing what we do and making the new behavior available to ourselves as good habits. Learning can be greatly accelerated by the process of teaching. When someone else already knows how to deal effectively with a new situation, that person can use language and demonstration to teach us the necessary new skills.

The word *teacher* usually brings to mind someone at the front of a classroom giving instructions. But this is not how the role gets performed at work. At work, teaching is most often performed as *coaching*, and it is something all of us try to do. We all want to influence how others act—we send verbal and nonverbal messages about this almost constantly:

"Max, get off the phone!"

"Could you bring these materials to me in batches of 20 instead of in various piles?"

"Hey, dummy, you just backed over a case marked 'Fragile'!"

"It would sure help if you would put this raw data into a scatter diagram."

Of course, we aren't always successful at getting the responses we would like. If we were all more effective as coaches, a lot more learning would occur in the workplace.

The first step to becoming more effective as a coach involves learning how to get the other person's attention. Structuring a message so that it penetrates another human being's nervous system is not easy.

Our nervous system processes millions of bits of information every moment. Scientific measurements have shown that the brain can process at least a quarter-million bits of data per second from each eye, so to compile a three-dimensional image in our minds, we must process at least a half a million bits of data per second. Add to this all the things we hear and smell and touch and taste, and we know that the nervous system is processing far more than a million bits of data per second. Since our brains seem remarkably capable of noticing what is going on around us, why is getting someone's attention such a problem?

The answer lies in the way people *prioritize* incoming data. Because the nervous system deals with so much information, it needs a very fast way of sorting out the messages that are most important and that deserve further consideration. Apparently, most people put all this information together in chunks and make decisions about whether each chunk is important, at a rate of about three times per second! The data requiring further attention are selected and held in short-term memory for three to five seconds. Thus, the first step in successful coaching is to structure our messages so that the recipient selects them out of the mass of incoming information and holds them in short-term memory.

Each of us is just one more droplet in a rainstorm of information falling on the people around us. All of us ignore most of this information rainfall; we would come psychologically unglued if we didn't. Each of us decides which information goes into short-term memory on the basis of whether it indicates a *need for change*. Our first question seems to be, "Is there some change I need to make to sustain my existence in this particular environment?" Data that do not imply the necessity for *immediate* change can be—and usually are—ignored.

Two Ways To Ask for Change

The signals that require us to change are transmitted on one of two channels: *threats* and *opportunities*. Threats mean we must change to sustain our survival or condition of well-being. We notice that a tire has blown on our automobile; we smell smoke in our office; we see that our rival is raising his hand to ask a question about our presentation. By contrast, opportunity signals indicate a chance to pursue our life concerns: food, an attractive person or a chance to make points for a job promotion. Thus, if we want to get another person's attention, we have two options—we can threaten, or we can present an opportunity.

In both cases, we are requiring someone to change. Human beings prefer not to change, however. As the nervous system scans the environment, it hopes to find that no change is required. We don't want to find anything that threatens our well-being or needs improvement. Change messages challenge the sense of well-being and thus create stress.

We must keep this in mind because we need to find a way to ask for change that creates as little stress as possible. If learning is the objective, stress is not a friend. As the previous chapter explained, stress causes downshift in the brain and slows or stops our capacity to explore new behaviors.

What are our options? It should be obvious that we are most likely to avoid downshift if we transmit messages on the *opportunity channel* rather than on the *threat channel*. The change messages that we send fall into one of four categories: *punishment, negative feedback, encouragement* and *advice*. Each has different effects on behavior. We can tell which channel our associates think we are using by looking at the *effects* of our communication.

Four Forms of Feedback

Punishment messages cause a particular behavior to stop. If we were to chart the frequency of a behavior being punished, the chart would show a rapid downward curve in frequency. The behavior falls off because the performer has interpreted our message as a painful consequence of that behavior. The performer stops the behavior to avoid the pain of another such message.

Notice that the type of message is defined by the *effect* it causes, *not* by the sender's intention. We may not have intended a comment about another person's work to be a threat or an assault on that person's self-esteem. We may have intended only to offer what we thought was helpful advice. But if the response we get is a rapid

Four Forms of Feedback

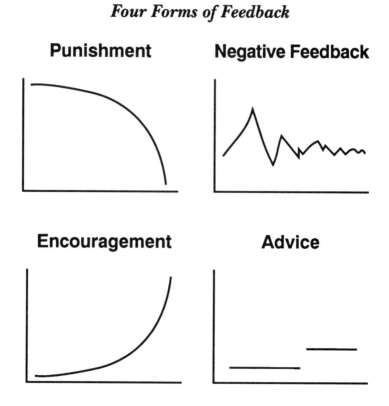

© 1992 American Consulting & Training, Inc.

reduction in the frequency with which the person does (or even attempts) the work, then the person is interpreting the message as punishment. None of us can fully control the meanings that listeners find in our messages. To know how other people interpret our message, we need to watch their behavior. If the behavior about which we sent the message drops off rapidly, it's safe to assume that the message was interpreted as punishment, even if that was not our intention.

It is important to know when we have been perceived as punishing, because punishment usually provokes vengeance. When the punished person has stopped some behavior, that person has energy left over to invest in trying to get even. Working relationships are almost always damaged whenever one of us inflicts punishment.

As soon as we notice that we have been mistakenly interpreted as punishing, we must start looking for opportunities to repair the relationship. Sometimes this means apologizing and explaining our intentions—but this may only make the other person more uncomfortable. Often it's best to evaluate what we did and wait for another opportunity to deliver our message more effectively.

Negative Feedback, another use of punishment, has a different overall effect: it stabilizes behavior. Rockets are guided by negative feedback. After a rocket is launched on its trajectory, various conditions cause it to go off track. When it does, the rocket's controllers send a signal saying, "No!" When the rocket turns back toward the desired track, the ground crew stops sending the "No" signal. With this series of "whacks" every time the rocket gets off course, it can be moved along the desired path.

Most of us get large doses of this kind of message as children. Our parents, teachers and siblings develop this habit because it's how they were taught, and because they need a way to coach us during our early years when we cannot understand language. We get our hands slapped by someone saying, "No!" So the first word that most children learn to say is "no."

As we move out of the Role Set of our families, we take on a new Role Set at school and finally at work. As we described in Chapter 1, our Role Set surrounds us with a few people who pay attention to our performance and *whack* us when they are disappointed. We go through life with these intimate social structures and their negative feedback. They teach us to internalize the feedback. Then we can go on *whacking* ourselves even when no one else is around. This gets us a reputation as "reliable adults."

The undesirable side effect of negative feedback is that it works too well. In addition to learning the desired behavior, the performer also has learned that experimentation—learning—will be painful. The stabilized pattern of behavior is seen as a sort of sanctuary from which the performer is not willing to budge. Furthermore, even the stable behavior is accompanied by all the stressful memories of how it was learned. When we stabilize behavior through negative feedback, we often get a performer who is in a permanent state of downshift, and it is difficult to get that behavior to change. If you are in an organization where learning is required, negative feedback will not create the appropriate environment.

Encouragement (a.k.a. positive reinforcement), the third type of change message, causes a behavior to increase in frequency. This effect is the direct opposite of punishment. If we were to chart the frequency of the encouraged behavior, we would get a rapidly rising curve. In this case, the behavior is increasing because the performer sees the message as a pleasant consequence of the behavior. The performer repeats the behavior to get more of the payoff.

The word encouragement connotes giving people courage to do more of the same performance. The message could be verbal—a compliment that specifically recognizes the performance—but it could also be a dollar bill, a lottery ticket or a finger pointing to a finished piece of work and a large smile. It could be applause or a pat on the back.

Encouragement is the most useful coaching tool. It is a way of repeatedly drawing positive attention to the goals of our working relationships—of keeping expectations clear. There is very little risk of hurting anyone when using encouragement. Furthermore, encouragement is relatively rare in most work environments, and most of us are so starved for it that the message has an unusually powerful effect whenever it is received.

There is a potential side-effect to encouragement, however. Whenever people start to do more of one behavior, they must borrow energy from some other behavior. Often, a person borrows energy from another behavior that we also want. So, instead of getting the whole performance we desire, we get more of part of it at the expense of other parts. For instance, we might compliment a workmate for keeping a clean desk. The next thing we know, the performer is spending more time keeping the desk clean than writing necessary reports.

When using positive reinforcement, it is important to keep the *whole* desired performance in mind. The most efficient way to do this is to talk with one another about Performance Plans. When we are able to keep encouragement within the context of the entire performance that teammates are depending upon, we find ways to borrow energy from behaviors that don't matter or are counter-productive. This is a double win—more of what is wanted, less of what is not.

Encouragement, within the context of commonly understood objectives, is the essence of good coaching relationships.

Advice, the fourth type of change communication, causes the listener to transfer energy deliberately from one behavior to another. Punishment and encouragement, remember, only affect the frequency of behavior. Advice actually causes the form of behavior to change.

Advice is an especially efficient way to modify behavior. It can stop undesirable behavior and transfer the energy invested in it to desirable behavior. That is the effect we want most when we coach.

Unfortunately, the most effective means of giving advice is not commonly understood. Most of our intended advice fails; it is usually interpreted as punishment. Compared to encouragement, advice carries much more risk of hurting the coaching relationship.

Many of us know this from experience. We remember working relationships that started well but turned sour. Initially, the relationship felt mutually respectful and supportive, but eventually it began showing signs of irritation, then resentment and finally open hostility. Both we and the other people probably were puzzled by this. Everyone's intentions were positive, but somehow the relationships became burdensome, a continuous struggle. We could only see one another "getting stuck" or "not doing it right." And the more advice we gave or got, the worse the relationships became.

Such memories are evidence of the risks in giving advice. Even where objectives are clearly understood and shared, poorly given advice poisons relationships with subtle forms of punishment. This problem can be avoided, and ways to do it are covered later in this chapter. But as we shall see, opportunities for giving effective advice are always limited.

Choose the Opportunity Channel

Remember that information regarding change is received on one of two channels: threat or opportunity. It should be obvious that punishment and negative feedback arrive on the threat channel. Such messages do get people's attention and provoke response, which is one reason we're so tempted to use them. At least in the short term, we get undesirable behavior to stop. But using the threat channel also damages our working relationships and causes downshift. These messages do not create environments for learning.

Instead, they just provoke old habits. Among the old habits are likely to be patterns of behavior that help people get away from those who threaten, or that satisfy a desire for vengeance.

The other two types of change message—encouragement and advice—tend to be received in the hearer's nervous system on the *opportunity channel.* It's important to ensure that this does, in fact, happen—that advice is not seen as punishment. Messages arriving on the opportunity channel are less stressful on the nervous system and increase the probability that the message will be received by a whole brain—one capable of exploring, choosing and perfecting new behaviors.

Rules and Tactics for Giving Encouragement

Encouragement is the type of coaching message we'll use most, and it is the easiest to do. Encouragement runs the least risk of being misunderstood and thereby damaging working relationships; and it is not likely to cause downshift. Encouragement can be used with colleagues who are not doing enough of what we expect and depend upon, and it can be used to get even more from those who are already doing a lot of what we want. Encouragement also can be offered in sincerity to people we like and people we don't.

Our workmates will increase the frequency of their behavior for two primary reasons. First, they will see our messages as a source of pleasure—our recognition, approval and other rewards make them feel good. Second, they'll probably believe that by repeating the behavior, they can sustain or increase their pleasure. Our messages of encouragement must create a connection in our associate's mind between pleasure and the desired behavior.

Pleasure and *reward* are very general terms. The variety of specific ways in which people seek these things is enormous and changes constantly for each individual. This is the only challenge of using encouragement. The way we deliver encouraging messages cannot be identical for all our workmates; nor can it remain the same for any one person very long. Some creativity and sensitivity on our part will be required.

Following the Six Rules for Encouragement can increase the probability that our encouragement will cause people to increase the frequency of behaviors we believe are crucial to cooperative success.

Six Rules for Encouragement

1. Specific

2. Pure

3. Positive

4. Immediate

5. Frequent

6. Irregular

Six Rules for Encouragement

Be Specific

This is the most important rule. We must describe exactly the behavior that we are trying to encourage. It is important not to use generalizations such as, "you're really good," or "it's really great to have you on the team." This type of talk is not encouragement. It is not related to a performer's specific behavior. Unless the performer is able to associate particular actions with our message and its pleasurable meanings, the message is unlikely to serve as encouragement.

Performers must understand precisely how they earned the message and believe that it's possible to earn that message again. It is this possibility that drives the message through the opportunity channel and gets the performers' attention. This internal process does not begin until performers understand what behavior creates this possibility for more rewards.

We might say, for example, "Thank you for following the new format in reporting your expenses. It will greatly speed up the reimbursement process." Or we could point to a chart in a report and say, "That is really good." The pointing makes clear what part of the report we are acknowledging and approving.

Almost all failures in delivering encouragement are associated with a failure to follow this first rule. It is extremely important. When we go around being positive in nonspecific ways, we are often seen as *backslappers*, *cheerleaders* and *air-heads*. Mindless cheer is not encouragement.

Keep Encouragement Pure

Typically, encouragement is given in a mixed fashion. For example, "This proposal for the new-product review process is very good. You've been comprehensive in addressing all the issues. The table of contents, index and glossary really help us find our way around the proposal and suggest a way of making our language consistent as we work on new products. But the report will need some graphics to make it truly readable." This is mixed feedback. Even though the compliments were quite specific and outnumber the suggestion at the end, an hour later the proposal writer is likely to remember the suggestion more than anything else. (In fact, as we'll see when examining the rules for giving advice, the writer will most likely remember that we looked over the report very carefully and were disappointed. Our message becomes a vague memory of disapproval in the hearer's mind.) When we mix encouragement and advice, the advice is most often what is really heard.

When we give bad news and good news at once, bad news seems to take priority. That's what gets our workmate's attention. Another way to say this is that if we transmit on the threat channel and the opportunity channel simultaneously, we'll only be heard on the threat channel. The threat message is more of an emergency.

We rarely see a performance that is perfect. The parts of a performance that usually capture our attention are the failures. The purity rule asks us for self-discipline—to notice and name *only* the parts that are done well and are, in fact, desirable. Do not mix messages by simultaneously talking about things that need change or improvement. When we mix the message, we lose the opportunity to deliver encouragement.

Focus on the Positive

Only encourage desirable behavior. We often accidentally encourage behaviors that we do not want. When we have extra time, for example, we sometimes step in to help workers who don't work quickly enough—this rewards them for working slowly. Sometimes our colleagues have energy tied up in personal problems with other workers. By spending a lot of time with them in sympathetic problem solving, we might accidentally wind up rewarding them for perpetuating the problem. It's their excuse for the pleasure of our company.

It is a good idea to spend most of our time giving attention and approval to the best performers on the team. By focusing encouragement on those who are doing well, those doing less well learn what we expect and how we reward top performance when we get it. Furthermore, good performers are often the people who, with a little encouragement, are able to give us the greatest return on our messages. They already know how to do what we want, and they can do more, sometimes more easily than anyone else on the team. Don't hesitate to use encouragement more frequently with the best performers.

Encourage Immediately

Encourage a performer immediately after the performance. The sooner we can offer encouragement, the better. For one thing, this makes it easier for performers to associate the encouragement with their own behavior. There's little possibility of confusion. This timing rule helps us achieve some of the specificity we were reaching for with Rule 1. But the main reason for the timing rule is to get inside the 30-minute time-frame in which the emotional brain operates (as described in Chapter 9). Habits must be rewarded right away to get stronger.

Often, the good performance of others doesn't come to our attention until hours or even weeks afterward. We may see such performances in a report, or hear someone else describing them in a meeting. Our encouragement can still have some power if we go as quickly as we can to the performers and let them know that their work has just come to our attention.

Encourage Frequently

Everyone should be able to find at least five good performances by their teammates every day, and to make a point of offering encouragement. The workplace really starts to cook when we start doing this at least 20 times a day! (We can make up a tally sheet and put this task into a Breakthrough System, by the way.)

Encouragement doesn't require any big ceremony. It can be as quick as pointing a finger and saying "Wow!" It can be saying "thank you" with full eye contact. It can be as simple as putting a smiling face on a good report. Twenty encouragements might take as little as four minutes a day.

It also helps to offer encouragement more frequently in the early stages of a performer's effort, to increase a behavior and to offer it less frequently as time passes. This procedure is called "thinning the schedule of reinforcement." It helps performers take over the task of encouraging themselves. Decreasing the frequency of encouragement does not mean, however, that we should ever stop. We need to let one another know that we appreciate reliable and enduring performance.

Frequency is important for two reasons. First, if a lot of rewards are flying around, all the team members have good reason to believe that they can earn some. Secondly, when people see others offering encouragement often, they stop being surprised by it. It doesn't seem to be unusual behavior that is driven by a peculiar motive. When we see one another doing enough encouraging, we come to notice that it is specifically related to good work. There isn't anything strange about it; it's just the way things are (and always should have been). Frequency combined with specificity make encouragement more likely to be perceived as credible and sincere.

Encourage Irregularly

It's important that we not encourage on a regular schedule. Encouragement should not be absolutely related to every performance, nor should it happen at the same time every day. It should come as a bit of a surprise.

Regular encouragement after every performance builds dependency in the performer. The performer counts on the coach to provide the encouragement and interprets its regularity as a sign of how important the performance is to the coach. As soon as the coach fails to offer the regular encouragement, the message becomes, "This performance doesn't matter anymore." So the performer stops doing it.

If we offer encouragement irregularly, performers begin to take some responsibility for encouraging themselves during the good performances we miss. Performers begin to say to themselves such things as: "Well, there was another good one, I'm sure, and you missed it, but it was a good one."

The coaching task is complete when performers internalize the process of encouragement and say to themselves, "I have learned to do the behavior; I continue to do the behavior; and I even take on the responsibility for coaching and encouraging myself as I do it well."

This is what we accomplish when we follow all Six Rules for Encouragement.

If we reflect on our successes in getting others to do more of what we want them to do, we usually discover that we are following these six rules. If we intend to be encouraging, but our associates fail to perceive us that way, we should return to these rules to assess what is going wrong. It's usually best to start at the top of the list—violations of Rules 1 and 2 account for most of our failures.

Tactics for Encouragement

Encouragement is always most effective when it conforms to the six rules listed on page 231, but there are many ways to package and deliver the message, including *Catch Them Doing Something Right*; *Arrangements*; *Sweet Surprises*; and *Contracts*.

Catch Them Doing Something Right

This is a basic compliment. Be on the lookout for people who have found solutions to problems, who are increasing the productivity we count on or who are holding their performances absolutely steady. Frequently flash approval for these performances, both verbally and nonverbally. This lets people know that we are paying attention to the things we said were important, that we are noticing their contributions and that we care. Do not hesitate to give thanks. It is a way of reminding one another that we are in dependent relationships and that we appreciate one another's support. When we follow the Six Rules for Encouragement, we can never overuse this tactic. (If we don't use the six rules, we risk sounding insincere.)

Arrangements

A second very effective tactic is to get others to deliver encouraging messages. In a meeting, for example, we might present a recommendation with overheads and handouts that our team has helped prepare. Somebody in the audience says, "Great graphics. I've never seen this relationship of the information before, and it really makes clear what the issues are. Beautiful work." Of course, we'll probably take this encouragement personally, and we should—we're part of the team that prepared this presentation. But we may also know that the charts were the idea of one member of the team who is not present at the meeting. So we say to the person offering the compliment, "Thank you. Mary was the one who came up with that idea. I would really appreciate it if you would drop by her cubicle after our meeting and let her know how much you liked it. I will share the compliment with her, too, but hearing it from you would be very encouraging." This is making an Arrangement.

Sweet Surprises

Encouragement need not always be a verbal message. Sometimes it is a tangible reward of some type. If someone performs in an extraordinary way, we can acknowledge that with a special reward. As soon as the results have been completed and delivered, try staging a surprise awards ceremony.

A list of rewards called "Tosti's Taxonomy" can be found on pages 237–238. Donald Tosti asked people in organizations, "What are the real rewards here? What things have been given to people as rewards for good work? What do you wish would be given to you when you do good work?" Tosti organized these into a variety of categories.

Notice that only one of the categories involves monetary rewards. Many of the items included here are perceived as significant awards, and are easily within our power to offer as Sweet Surprises—especially with a little assistance from a manager.

Contracting

A fourth tactic is called Contracting: making a deal ahead of time that a specific reward will be given when a certain task or goal is achieved. We might say, for example: "If you give me those devices a week earlier than scheduled, I'll give you my tickets to the ball game." Again, Tosti's Taxonomy can stimulate our imagination for picking a reward.

Some people think that this is a form of bribery and is unethical. We should never use any form of contracting that makes us feel immoral. There are, however, many ways to use contracting that fit everyone's system of values.

To summarize: encouragement is the safest coaching strategy to use. Using it involves lots of experimentation. We must be prepared for the possibility that what we consider to be a reward may not be so for others. We must watch for the responses to see whether our messages are being received according to our intentions.

Remember, also, that encouragement is not a gift that we give to others. It's something the performer has earned. It is something that we *owe* because we depend on the good performance of others. The mentality of paying our dues by giving encouragement gives our working relationships their proper tenor.

Tosti's Taxonomy

A Checklist of Incentives

Regarding _____
(Name of Person)

Recognition

- Praise
- Awards
- Certification of accomplishment
- Formal public acknowledgments (e.g., testimonials and plaques)
- Informal acknowledgments (i.e.,"pat on the back")
- Letters of appreciation
- Publicity (e.g., personal notes in the company newsletter or the "employee of the month" postings)
- Selection to represent group at meetings

Tangible Rewards

- Cash bonuses
- Commissions
- Profit sharing
- Piecework pay
- Merit increases
- Prizes (e.g., TVs, trips, etc.)
- Lunch on the company
- Company stock
- Paid trips to professional meetings
- Company donations to charity or college fund in employee's name
- Increased "fringe benefits" (e.g., life insurance, use of company car)

Social Activities

- Talking to fellow employees (e.g., work or "coffee" groups)
- Going to lunch with the gang
- Going to company outing or parties
- Going to company organized recreational activities (e.g., bowling team)
- "Shooting the breeze" with the boss
- Having the boss listen to problems with interest
- Dinner (lunch , drinks or just coffee) with the boss (and spouse)

Job Responsibilities

- Opportunity for more self management
- More power to decide and/or implement (i.e., scope)
- More frequent decision making or participation in decision making
- More frequent requests to provide input for decisions
- Greater opportunity to schedule time (e.g., set own priorities)
- Greater access to information

Job Tasks

- Assignment of new duties
- Vertical redesign of present job (i.e., "see job through to the end")
- Relief from aversive duties
- Change in ratio of preferred duties
- Frequent changes of duties
- Assignment of preferred work partners
- Approval of job-related requests
- Rapid follow-up by boss on job-related problems
- Opportunity for advanced training

Status Indicators

- Larger work area
- A promotion
- More private office
- Receiving more or newer equipment
- Status symbols (e.g., window, carpeting, nameplate, plants, key to executive lounge, better desk, etc.)
- Invitations to "high level" meetings
- A new title
- Being placed in a special category (e.g., tenured)

Tosti's Taxonomy–continued

Incentive Feedback
- Increased knowledge of quantitative outputs
- Graphs of progress
- Receiving knowledge of effect of individual performance (e.g., in accomplishing group goals, solving boss's problem, helpfulness to others, productivity, etc.)
- Receiving knowledge on quality of work
- Being informed of eventual results of output (i.e., getting the "big picture")
- Receiving "fan mail" (e.g., customer compliments)

Personal Activities
- Doing "goof-off" behaviors that are permitted in a work environment (e.g., going to the drinking fountain)
- Doing "goof-off" behaviors that are usually proscribed in a work environment (i.e., working crossword puzzles)
- Taking longer break or receiving additional breaks or longer lunch times
- Leaving work earlier
- Time off with or without pay
- Privileges (e.g., phone calls, opportunity to travel, reserved parking, etc.)
- "Creative" activities (e.g., work on inventions or publications)

Relief from Aversive Policies or Procedures
- Exemption from time clocks
- Exemption from selected company control policies
- Exemption from close supervision
- Relief from threat of dismissal, loss of pay or probationary status

Relief from Aversive Work Environment
- Better lighting
- Move to less noisy location
- Transfer from uncongenial work mates or supervisor
- Move to warmer or cooler work area
- Move closer to "comfort" facilities (e.g., restrooms, cafeteria, coffee pot)

Tosti, Dr. Donald, "A Taxonomy of Educational Reinforcement," (with Roger Addison), *Educational Technology*, September, 1979. Reprinted with permission.

Rules and Tactics for Giving Advice

We have many more opportunities to encourage than we ever have to offer advice. And making mistakes when offering advice can harm our working relationships—advice at the wrong time is usually taken as punishment.

On the other hand, advice is a wonderful way to share our experience with others. When others like our ideas and find them useful, it encourages us. It makes us want to find more ways to be helpful. Everyone's learning accelerates—coaches and coachees—when we are allowed to show one another the short-cuts to success that we have already discovered.

Six Rules for Giving Advice

---

1. Current (undesirable behavior)

2. Desirable behavior

3. Pure

4. Just before useful

5. Focused

6. Look for new behavior

Six Rules for Giving Advice

The rules that govern the successful delivery of advice are as follows:

Describe the Behavior That Is Undesirable

Before attempting to give advice, we must be clear *in our own minds* about what we find undesirable in the current behavior.

It is best to define our dissatisfaction in terms of the *results* or *consequences* we think the behavior is causing. We may be irritated by the fact that one of our colleagues didn't get back from lunch at 1 p.m. sharp, for example. So what? If we're just getting hung up on the rules, we should consider dropping the matter. Maybe it's not a real problem. But if the tardiness actually disrupted our own performance—made it impossible for us to get information that customers expected us to have, for example—then the issue is substantive. Focusing on consequences is the first step in defining the issue about which we want to give advice, and it also helps us check that our motives are appropriate.

Often, we won't need to spend time discussing these consequences; they'll be quite obvious. But we must be prepared to name the *results* we find undesirable, just in case we discover that the other person really isn't noticing them. This is also a way to make sure that we are not talking about the problem with a downshifted brain. Analyzing the situation in terms of consequences requires our cognitive brain to be active, and this is especially important when giving advice. Going into the situation downshifted guarantees that the message will not be received as advice.

Describe the Behavior That Is Desirable

When giving advice, we must describe the results we want from the other person's behavior. We may also describe and/or demonstrate specific procedures that we believe will produce the desired results, but that isn't always necessary.

In the tardiness case previously mentioned, our desired result is to be able to get information for customers any time after 1 p.m. If we must get this information from the person who isn't always back from lunch on time, we're obviously suggesting a specific procedure for this person: get back at 1 p.m. sharp.

We may need to practice saying this advice message. We might write it down first, or go to some private place and listen to ourself say it. It helps to remember that we aren't building an argument. We don't have to be "right." The other person doesn't have to be "wrong." If we remember this, we can state our perception of the problem as simply as we can. It is especially important to make sure that we are not exaggerating anything. It always helps to be as specific as possible and to minimize the problem as much as possible. It isn't a good idea to say, "I don't *ever* seem to be able to get the information I need from you right after lunch—I *always* have to wait and then call the customers back. They act all upset and then I feel stupid." It is better to say, "I failed to answer a customer's question because I couldn't get the information I needed from you—you weren't at your work station. I think I should have answered that customer's question immediately."

When we follow Rules 1 and 2, all we are doing is making our perception of the problem clear. Remember that it is only our perception. We have some data, but we may not know the whole story. Or we might find that our perception is shaped by some assumptions that are not appropriate. Clearly stating our perception invites the other person to correct us if necessary, and of course they often will.

In the tardiness case, the other person may apologize for the inconvenience and then explain that she was busy giving CPR to a heart attack victim in the cafeteria. If this was a singular event, obviously the problem is not worth discussing any further. (We congratulate our associate for helping the victim.) But if this is the third time we've had our problem with customers this week, we must share the facts with the other person and be more specific about suggesting a prompt return from lunch. Some of us develop a habit of apologizing and offering an excuse to avoid changes that we should make to honor our working relationships. Most of us can recognize this habit in others, and when we do, we should persist in making clear what we want.

A lot of other things could be going on in the situation, however. What if work schedules have been changed and we're supposed to be calling someone *else* after 1:00 p.m.? What if the other person has been answering our questions as a favor, when in fact we have the information in the manuals that we are supposed to know how to use? Rules 1 and 2 aren't going to make it possible for us to demand or sell behavior change—that's not their intent. The rules only help us enter the relationship in a way that quickly validates or corrects our partial perceptions of reality. Maybe this will move everyone in the direction of better cooperation.

Keep Advice Pure

Just as in encouragement, when the time comes to give advice, we must stay with our advice. It is unnecessary to "candy-coat it" or make it "schmoozy." We just have to stick to the point.

Some people believe it's possible (and preferable) to slip people an *advice sandwich*—a message between two slices of fluff. The method is to start by saying nice things, stick it to 'em, then end on a positive note. This sandwich method easily leads the listener to confusion, and we'll be lucky if that's the worst that happens. Many people see this method as sneaky, manipulative, fork-tongued, two-faced. Why risk damaging our reputation for integrity?

We just ask for the specific result we want, as reasonably as we can. The time to "say nice things" is when we get the results that we want. Then we'll be doing more than being nice, we'll be offering encouragement.

Offer Advice Just Before It Can Be Used

This is the most important rule for giving advice! Timing is everything. The other person should be able to use our advice within the next 30 minutes. We can get away with a lot of different communication styles—from gentle to blunt—if we offer advice when the other person can actually use it.

The rule isn't hard to follow for repetitive tasks. We can interrupt between performances and say, "Do the next one like this." The other person has an immediate opportunity to use the advice. Often in such situations, others take the advice so quickly and so well that we have trouble appreciating that we've just witnessed the miracle of learning. Follow up with encouragement, and the new behavior will go into the bag of habits—right into the protein of the emotional brain—very quickly! That's the perfect response to advice: the old behavior stops, and the energy that was used to do it is transferred to the new behavior.

How does this rule affect the way that we give advice in the case of the tardiness discussed earlier? We may be tempted to talk to the person as soon as she returns from lunch—right after we've had the problem and it is fresh in our mind. But wait! The behavior we are trying to change is the person's late return from lunch. The person won't have a chance to use our advice until tomorrow. The rule says that we should catch the person just before lunch the next day.

In both cases, it's pretty easy to know when the person will be able to use the advice. The hard cases will arise in Troubleshooting tasks that come up unexpectedly and require immediate response. We won't know when our associate's next opportunity to take our advice will come; nor will the other person have much time to take advice when the occasion does arise. Such situations call for a tactic called Rehearsal/Fire Drill, which is explained later.

This timing rule makes clear that the opportunities for giving advice are rarer than most of us have noticed. Many of us just can't wait—we're sure that the other person will need the advice, even though they can't use it right away. We are often encouraged in this belief by people's apparently thankful response. "Thanks. I needed that!" is what they say. So we think we've done all right. Realize instead that these brave, adult, "I learn from failure" responses are often habits for escaping the moment. We're getting a response from the emotional brain, not the whole brain. Learning is not actually taking place. The proof is in the listener's failure to transfer energy out of the old behavior into the new one.

This is not an easy rule to follow. Some people call it the "Tooth-Mark-on-the-Tongue Rule." We bite our tongues in silence every time we realize that the other person isn't going to be able to use our advice in the next few minutes. Advice at the wrong time is usually remembered later as a message of punishment. If we can't give advice at the right time, it's usually best not to give it at all.

Keep Advice Focused

This rule is related to Rules 1 and 2. We must be very specific about the performance we are trying to take the energy *from* and the performance toward which we want the energy to *move*. In particular, we must avoid the *shotgun approach*. It is ineffective to present people with a long list of things that we need to fix and correct.

Effective advice-giving takes thought and preparation. Even then, it's always a little risky. It's important that we not waste advice on the small stuff. We must pick the key behaviors that most affect other people's success in helping the team meet its common goals. These are the performances where learning will provide the greatest payoff. We then focus our few opportunities for advice on the key performances.

Look for the New Behavior

This rule reminds us to watch for the effects of our advice-giving. It also reminds us never to give hit-and-run advice. If we're offering advice just before it can be used, this rule won't be difficult to follow. We can just stand by to see whether the new behavior is adopted.

Observing this rule will probably make us believers in the other five—especially the timing rule. We'll notice that when we break the rules, people don't take our advice. They start finding ways to avoid situations in which they could use advice. Instead of fixing a presentation as we had advised, for instance, they might delegate the task to someone else, or get sick the night before, so that someone else has to do it. Often people withdraw energy and actually stop the very performances that we think we are helping them improve. We may also notice changes in our working relationships if we ignore these rules. Others will not just avoid the specific performances that we advise them about; they will begin to avoid us, too.

As we learn to watch for this pattern of avoidance, we may be shocked to see how often our advice is being taken as punishment. Usually the reason is that we are not following the timing rule. A little reflection on our own experience can usually help us understand what is happening.

When we get advice that we can't use right away, we tend to forget the specific suggestions for change our adviser offered.

Instead, we only remember that someone noticed and disapproved of our performance. The moment of advice is only remembered as an event of failure and disapproval. But when we have a chance to use advice immediately, we get to prove, at least to ourselves, that we can perform at the desired level. Our instant improvement may also earn immediate encouragement from others. These possibilities can make the memory of advice a memory of success. And nothing breeds ambition like success. We're much more likely to follow the advice in the future.

Standing by to see how our message of advice has been taken also gives us the chance to correct misunderstandings. Sometimes our suggestions are not clearly made. Sometimes our associates misunderstand because they are under stress and unable to learn. We can often get our coaching job done just by being patient and sincere in our support. Sometimes, we'll just need to make note of what went off track and wait for a better opportunity to try again.

Tactics for Giving Advice

As with encouragement, the general rules for giving advice apply to all cases. The *tactics* for giving advice are many, however, including *Just-in-Time Advice (JITA)*, *Lead 'em to Water*, the *Delayed Fuse* and the *Fire Drill*.

Just-in-Time Advice

We give JITA when we step into a situation and interrupt, offer advice and stand back to see whether the person can do it. We must keep offering the advice until the person gets it right. We demonstrate, draw pictures or do anything else necessary to clarify what we want, until we get the desired performance.

Just-in-Time Advice does not require a lot of time. When we get our timing right, these interruptions are often brief. Verbally, the advice might sound like this: "Please add a table of contents." Giving this advice while the person is working on the report makes it quick and efficient. Sometimes the advice is not even verbal—just tapping the person's shoulder to remind them of a step in the procedure. Often, little more is required.

Lead 'em to Water

A second tactic is called Lead 'em to Water. It comes from the old saying, "You can lead 'em to water, but you can't make 'em drink." Others control their own performances and that's as it should be. But we can set our associates up to take a drink of what we think is success.

We may notice that our associates are quoting the wrong prices for parts and services, for example, because they are using an outdated price sheet. The solution is to find and deliver the new price list. Or we may know that a colleague tends to do the steps of a procedure out of sequence. We can give the person a checklist. We can also lead people to water by taking them to watch someone who does their kind of work very well. In all cases, we are providing resources in such a way that others will have the right tools available when they are needed.

Delayed Fuse

The Delayed Fuse tactic is useful when our associate will have a predictable delay before the next opportunity to perform the task. Public presentations are a good illustration. Suppose a colleague comes to us immediately after a presentation and asks, "How did you like my presentation? How can I improve it?" First ask, "When will you be preparing for the next presentation?" When the person responds, "I'll be preparing for another next Monday afternoon," arrange to meet at that time. This arrangement is a Delayed Fuse. We might use this moment immediately after the presentation to mention the specific parts that we found especially effective. It's the time for encouragement, not advice. When people ask for advice at the wrong time, we are well advised to do our working relationship the favor of using a Delayed Fuse.

Others may not understand what we are doing the first time we use this tactic. They may ask, "Why don't you tell me now?" Our response should not be devious; we can use the opportunity to teach the rule for giving advice just when it can be used. We should ask the person to cooperate as an experiment, and see how it works.

Sometimes a person can use a little help with a presentation but doesn't ask. If we can find out when the person will prepare for the next one, we can set up a reminder in our calendar to visit at that time. This is another form of the Delayed Fuse.

Sometimes we will not be able to arrange to be with the person at the appropriate time to give advice. In that case, it would be a good idea to write out our advice and put it in an envelope marked, "Read before you plan the charts for your next presentation." Hand the envelope over, and explain to the person why it's important to wait before reading the instructions.

Rehearsal/Fire Drill

The last of the tactics covered here is Rehearsal or Fire Drill. It's useful when the next opportunity to use advice is *unpredictable*. It is especially useful when we are giving advice to people who perform Troubleshooting tasks.

The best we can do when the next required performance of a task is unpredictable is to create an immediate need for the performance. Explain or demonstrate the desired performance, then role-play the situation—hold a "Fire Drill."

In a situation where someone comes to us immediately after a presentation and asks for advice, instead of using a Delayed Fuse we can ask whether the person has time right then for a brief practice session. If so, we can offer advice and ask the person to try it. We can keep working with the presenter until the presentation improves, and then switch to encouragement, emphasizing the benefits of the new skill. The Rehearsal sets up an immediate opportunity for the other person to use our advice and turns out to be a powerfully effective and safe way of coaching any performance.

Of all the rules for giving advice, the most important is the timing rule. Don Tosti, whose research brought this rule to public attention, contributed genuinely fresh and brilliant ideas that can greatly improve everyone's ability to learn in the workplace.

Summary: First Be Your Own Coach

The best place to begin practicing the coaching skills of Encouragement and Advice is on ourselves.

It is surprising how few of us ever take the time to encourage ourselves—to carefully notice our own performance strengths. We operate on them as unconscious assumptions. Or we try to lift our own spirits and cover our sense of inadequacy with the empty slogans of cheerleading. Some of us even believe that dwelling on our strengths leads to the evils of pride. However, being specific, pure, immediate and frequent in recognizing our own strengths is actually one of the disciplines of genuine self-knowledge. It builds a sober self-confidence, nurtures a willingness to be responsible for ourselves, and makes us more attentive and appreciative of the strengths of others. Encouraging ourselves according to the rules and with the tactics discussed in this chapter is one of the secrets to rapid learning, the continuous development of social value and the enjoyment of life.

At least, we could stop punishing ourselves with poor advice! So many of us have learned the bad habit of indulging in self-criticism immediately following everything we do. And no criticism is ever as painful as the criticism we inflict on ourselves. We talk to ourselves as if we believe we must kick ourselves through the goal posts of life, and we kick so hard! What a relief it is when we still the inner voice of untimely advice!

When we learn to encourage our own strengths immediately after their display, and to reserve our advice until the moments just before challenging performance is required, many of us discover a whole new world of personal potential. Not only do we become better coaches for ourselves, we learn how to make better use of others as coaches. Vast new quantities of resources seem to become available—though, in fact, most of them have always been present and ignored. The acceleration of our own learning proves to us the validity of the rules for Encouragement and Advice. We become mature in understanding all the ways that Encouragement and Advice can affect our lives. And we become skilled in assisting others on the path to Breakthrough Performance.

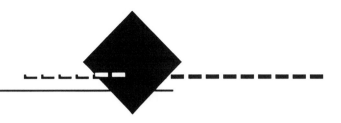

Endnotes

◆ ◆ ◆ ◆

Chapter 1

Bridges, William. *Job/Shift.* Menlo Park, California: Addison-Wesley Publishing Co., 1994.

Horsfal, A.B., and C.M. Arensberg. "Team Work and Productivity in a Shoe Factory," *Human Organization,* (August 1949).

Kahn, R.L., et al. *Organizational Stress: Studies in Role Conflict and Ambiguity.* Melbourne, Fl.: Robert Krieger Publishing Co., Inc., 1980.

Kahn, R.L. "Conflict, Ambiguity, and Overload: Three Elements in Job Stress." In *The Study of Organizations,* edited by Katz, D., R.L. Kahn, and J.S. Adams. San Francisco: Jossey-Bass, 1980.

Kanter, Donald L., and P.H. Mirvis. *The Cynical Americans: Living and Working in an Age of Discontent and Disillusion.* San Francisco: Jossey-Bass, 1989.

Katz, D., and R.L. Kahn. *The Social Psychology of Organizations.* 2nd ed. New York: Wiley & Sons, 1978.

Krugman, Paul. *Peddling Prosperity: Economic Sense & Nonsense in the Age of Diminished Expectations.* New York: Norton & Company, 1994.

249

Miller, F.B. "Situational Interactions, a Worthwhile Concept," *Human Organization.* (1958).

Schor, Juliet B. *The Overworked American: The Unexpected Decline of Leisure.* New York: BasicBooks, 1991.

Terkel, Studs. *Working: People Talk about What They Do All Day and How They Feel about What They Do.* New York: Avon Books, 1972.

Chapter 2

Behaviorism and the Bottom Line. A training film in which the Emery Air Freight story is told. Edward J. Feeney was the consultant involved in the project.

Daniels, William R. *Chain Gang: A Simulation for Teaching Breakthrough Systems (Manufacturing Emphasis).* Mill Valley: American Consulting & Training, Inc., 1989.

———. *Pentaspheres: A Simulation for Teaching Breakthrough Systems (Project Management Emphasis).* Mill Valley: American Consulting & Training, Inc., 1994.

Juran, J.M. *Juran on Planning for Quality.* New York: Free Press, 1988.

———. *Managerial Breakthrough,* New York: McGraw-Hill, 1964.

Kopelman, Richard E. "Improving Productivity Through Objective Feedback: A Review of the Evidence," *National Productivity Review,* (Winter 1982–83).

Chapter 3

Daniels, William R. *Breakthrough for Productivity: A Training Program for First Line Managers.* Mill Valley: American Consulting & Training, Inc., 1982.

———. *Performance Planning and Coaching: A Training Program for Middle Managers.* Mill Valley: American Consulting & Training, Inc., 1980.

Chapter 7

Daniels, William R. *How To Write Your Performance Plan.* Mill Valley: American Consulting & Training, Inc., 1985.

Kotter, John P. *Power and Influence.* New York: Free Press, 1985.

———. *The General Managers.* New York: Free Press, 1982.

———. *The Leadership Factor.* New York: Free Press, 1988.

Likert, Rensis. *The Human Organization: Its Management and Value.* New York: McGraw-Hill, 1967.

———. *New Patterns of Management.* New York: McGraw-Hill, 1961.

Chapter 8

Argyris, Chris. *Overcoming Organizational Defenses: Facilitating Organizational Learning.* Needham Heights, Mass.: Allyn and Bacon, 1990.

Daniels, William R. *Orchestrating Powerful Regular Meetings.* San Diego: Pfeiffer & Company, 1990.

———.*Group Power: A Manager's Guide to Conducting Task Forces.* San Diego: Pfeiffer & Company, 1986.

Schaffer, Robert H. *The Breakthrough Strategy: Using Short-Term Successes To Build the High Performance Organization.* New York: Ballinger, 1988.

Chapter 9

OptimaLearning-Barzak Educational Institute, Novato, California. Ivan Barzakov, Director.

Frijda, Nico H. *The Emotions: Studies in Emotion & Social Interaction,* London: Cambridge University Press, and Paris: Editions De La Maison Des Sciences De L'Homme, 1977.

Chapter 10

Connellan, Thomas K. *How To Improve Human Performance: Behaviorism in Business & Industry.* New York: Harper & Row, 1978.

Fournies, Ferdinand F. *Coaching for Improved Work Performance.* New York: Van Nostrand Reinhold Co., 1978.

Tosi, Henry L., and Stephen J. Carroll. *Management: Contingencies, Structure and Process.* New York: Wiley and Sons, 1976.

Tosi, Henry L., and W. Clay Hammer, eds. *Organizational Behavior & Management: A Contingency Approach.* Rev. ed. New York: Wiley and Sons, 1977.

Tosti, Donald, with Roger Addison. "A Taxonomy of Educational Reinforcement," *Educational Technology,* September, 1979.

Tosti, Donald. "Formative Feedback," *NSPI Journal,* (October 1978).

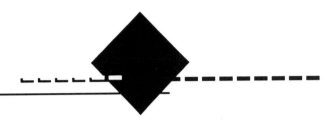

Index

◆ ◆ ◆ ◆